CONEY ISLAND THE PARACHUTE PAVILION COMPETITION

CONEY ISLAND THE PARACHUTE PAVILION COMPETITION

ZOË RYAN AND JONATHAN COHEN-LITANT, EDITORS

VAN ALEN INSTITUTE
PRINCETON ARCHITECTURAL PRESS

Published by
Princeton Architectural Press
37 East Seventh Street
New York, New York 10003

For a free catalog of books, call 1-800-722-6657.
Visit our Web site at www.papress.com.

"Coney Island: The Technology of the Fantastic" reproduced
by permission of the publisher from Rem Koolhaas,
Delirious New York: A Retroactive Manifesto for Manhattan
(New York: The Monacelli Press, 1997).
First published 1978 by Oxford University Press.

Editing: Linda Lee
Design: Paul Wagner

Special thanks to: Nettie Aljian, Sara Bader, Dorothy Ball,
Nicola Bednarek, Janet Behning, Becca Casbon,
Penny (Yuen Pik) Chu, Russell Fernandez, Peter Fitzpatrick,
Sara Hart, Jan Haux, Clare Jacobson, John King, Mark Lamster,
Nancy Eklund Later, Katharine Myers, Lauren Nelson Packard,
Scott Tennent, Jennifer Thompson, Joseph Weston, and
Deb Wood of Princeton Architectural Press
—Kevin C. Lippert, publisher

Library of Congress Cataloging-in-Publication Data

Coney Island : Parachute Pavilion competition / Zoë Ryan and
Jonathan Cohen-Litant, editors.
    p.   cm.
ISBN-13: 978-1-56898-623-4 (pbk. : alk. paper)
ISBN-10: 1-56898-623-8 (pbk. : alk. paper)
1. Parachute Pavillion (New York, N.Y.) 2. Coney Island
(New York, N.Y.) 3. Architecture—Competitions—New York
(State)—New York. 4. Carmody Groarke Hardie (Firm)
I. Ryan, Zoë. II. Cohen-Litant, Jonathan.
NA8450.C575 2007
725'.827—dc22
                                2006022740

CONTENTS

Coney Island is a legend, an "only in Brooklyn" slice of Americana. In its heyday, its beaches, boardwalk, Nathan's famous hotdogs, the Parachute Jump, the Cyclone Rollercoaster, and the Wonder Wheel were New York City's and America's favorite playground—it was the neighborhood that symbolized Brooklyn to the world.

The Cyclone's first steep drop still stuffs your heart into your stomach and froths it up like an egg cream. But times and tastes change. In the coming years, Coney Island will undergo some exciting changes that will preserve its cherished freakishness while ushering its fun-loving spirit into the twenty-first century.

The tremendous response to the Parachute Pavilion Open Ideas Competition proves that when it comes to Coney Island's future, the whole world wants to be a part of it. Entries came from places as diverse as Brooklyn itself: China, Japan, Poland, Russian, and, of course, England. With more than fifty entries from Brooklyn, we saw how our vibrant architecture and design community helps make it the creative capital of the United States.

Alongside the beautiful relighting of the Parachute Jump, the new pavilion will create a new focal point that perfectly embodies the Brooklyn attitude— brash, bold, and colorful and also cutting-edge, inviting, and useful. Just as Coney Island's Steeplechase Park and Dreamland symbolize a bygone era, the Parachute Jump and pavilion will be the icons of the Coney Island of tomorrow. With its themes of innovation and cultural activation, and as the bridge between the past and the future, the pavilion is on its way to becoming a true Brooklyn legend!

Marty Markowitz
Brooklyn Borough President

When the Society of Beaux-Arts Architects awarded its first Paris Prize in 1904, the goal of identifying promising young architects and providing them with an opportunity to broaden their skills through participating in a design competition—with a reward of European travel and education—was a new concept for Americans aspiring to practice architecture. For nine decades the society continued this tradition, even after the Beaux-Arts method and style lost favor to orthodox modernism.

To celebrate the centenary of the Paris Prize in 2004, the Van Alen Institute (VAI), successor to the society and its later incarnations, the Beaux-Arts Institute of Design and the National Institute for Architectural Education, initiated a new award, the New York Prize. The new prize, like the old, seeks to identify promising designers at an early stage in their career and has evolved to allow for both team recognition and international participation.

The New York Prize is awarded to an outstanding project or firm and was given this year to the winners of the Parachute Pavilion Open Ideas Competition. The winning team researched the idea of pavilions, and their essay, "Pavilion: Symbol of Recreation and Regeneration," published in this volume, delves into an architectural idea at the heart of the new prize—the potential for articulating how design and architecture affect the urban public realm today. Like Paris of 1904, New York today represents a vital setting for explorations of the city and design and is the perfect inspiration for competition subjects that range from buildings to open spaces to information systems that guide city visitors.

Sherida E. Paulsen
Chair, Van Alen Institute

Contemplating the future of Coney Island can be intimidating, given the richness of its legends and the sheer scale of its role in the psyche, the identity, of New York City. Yet for many of us, now is a critical moment for Coney Island. In 2003, Mayor Michael R. Bloomberg created the Coney Island Development Corporation (CIDC), which has resulted in a blueprint for Coney's future. As the chair of the CIDC, I hear it in the voices of community members, business people, and Coney Island enthusiasts almost a reverence, for Coney Island. All share a determination to recapture Coney's magic, a confidence that a renewed Coney can and must reinvent itself once again, and a recognition that Coney Island is on its way back.

The challenge of honoring Coney's past and maintaining its authenticity, while allowing new growth and changes, is the basis for CIDC's redevelopment plan. This same balance between nostalgia and vision informed the decision to seek as broad an array of ideas as possible for the development of a pavilion at the base of the iconic Parachute Jump. While only one component of the greater plans for Coney Island, the pavilion nevertheless has the potential to make a grand statement: Coney Island continues to forge ahead, while paying homage to and building upon its past.

I approached the Van Alen Institute with the belief that a global competition would send a strong signal about Coney's resurgence. The results of the pavilion competition surpassed my expectations—they are a testament to the sheer breadth of interest across the globe in Coney Island and the powerful brand identity it possesses. The range of ideas presented by the respondents, from the wacky to the beautiful, the imaginative to the innovative, embodies the very spirit of Coney Island itself. If only we could build them all!

Josh Sirefman
Chair, Coney Island Development Corporation

Design competitions, whether open or invited, single or multiple stages, have played a critical role in the regeneration of neighborhoods and cities worldwide. Competitions are complex processes that can help elevate the level of discourse, create public awareness of the importance of quality design, and result in concepts and built projects that are thought provoking and push the established boundaries—essential components of successful urban regeneration projects.

The Parachute Pavilion Open Ideas Competition was conceived as an inclusive and open process that would provide a platform for design excellence while also generating renewed interest in Coney Island, a historically and culturally rich neighborhood seeking to once again become a significant urban destination. The critical collaboration between the Van Alen Institute (VAI) and its city agency partners, the New York City Economic Development Corporation (ECD) and the Coney Island Development Corporation (CIDC), and the timing of the project to coincide with the announcement of a strategic plan for Coney Island proved to be essential factors in the success of the competition.

Since its inception in 1894, the Institute has sustained a century-long tradition of initiating some of New York's largest and most-inspired design competitions for sites ranging from Wall Street to Times Square, the East River to Queens Plaza, Governors Island to Pier 40, and Battery Park City to Coney Island. Most recently VAI has reached beyond New York with a competition for Philadelphia. The Institute's partnerships with New York City and with public and private agencies and organizations have generated a wealth of ideas with the goal of improving the quality of urban public life in New York and beyond.

In 1996 the Institute (formerly the Beaux-Arts Institute of Design and later the National Institute for Architectural Education) was renamed in honor of its founding member and benefactor, William Van Alen (1883–1954), architect of the Chrysler Building and the winner of VAI's prestigious Paris Prize design competition in 1908. Since then, the institute has continued to be a leading force promoting emerging and established talents in the fields of architecture, landscape architecture, and design.

It is this esteemed tradition that continues to inspire change in public spaces and reinforces the institute's mission as a think-tank dedicated to promoting design excellence within the public realm.

This publication celebrates the extraordinary response to the Parachute Pavilion Open Ideas Competition, the largest in the Institute's history. All 864 entries from forty-six countries are presented. These are from countries including the United States, Australia, Bangladesh, Bolivia, Canada, China, the Czech Republic, France, India, Ireland, Japan, Israel, Mexico, Poland, Russia, Thailand, Turkey, the United Kingdom, Uruguay, and Venezuela. Along with the winning projects, some of the most inventive ideas are presented within the ten following themes: (In)Suspense, Beachscape, Tactile TECH-Style, Coneyscope, Extending the Boardwalk, Beyond the Brief, Archi-types, Active (S)pace, Medium as Media, Take Away. These categories emphasize their key ideas and act as guides to exploring the projects. The quality and variety of the submissions is a testimony to the importance of design competitions in raising the bar for innovative thinking and design.

Competition Background

In summer 2004, VAI partnered with the CIDC to launch a competition to coincide with current CIDC planning initiatives for the regeneration of Coney Island. VAI directed this ambitious project for the design of a recreational pavilion to sit in the shadow of the famed Parachute Jump—an iconic reminder of Coney Island's historic past. The project is envisioned as a symbol of Coney Island's future and will play a key role in its ongoing revival.

The competition called for an all-season generator of activity, drawing the public onto the boardwalk, the beach, and Surf Avenue and to a new recreational destination. Throughout history pavilions have acted as paradigms of innovative design. They have also proven to be catalysts for animating parks, waterfronts, and urban districts by accommodating a myriad of recreational and commercial activities. The competition invited designers to stretch the limits of the traditional pavilion, both formally and programmatically, and asked for a concept that connected to both the history and future of Coney Island.

Top: Aerial view of Coney Island, 2005 / Bottom: Coney Island boardwalk, 2005

Aerial view of Coney Island showing competition site and Parachute Jump, 2005

Astroland Park, Coney Island, 2005

Process

In June 2005, 864 teams submitted their vision for the future Parachute Pavilion. The jury was held at the New York Aquarium at Coney Island and was comprised of design professionals, stakeholders, city officials, and local residents. Participants included Carol Hill Albert, co-owner of Astroland Park; Paola Antonelli, curator, Department of Architecture and Design, The Museum of Modern Art; Jon Benguiat, Director of Planning and Development, Brooklyn Borough President's Office; Mark Hacker, Director of Development, Rockwell Group; Michael A. Manfredi, principal, Weiss/Manfredi; Sheryl Robertson, Coney Island resident and local community organizer; Jennifer Siegal, principal and founder of Office of Mobile Design; and Julius Spiegel, Brooklyn Borough Commissioner, New York City Department of Parks and Recreation.

Throughout the jury process, all designs remained anonymous until the final selection was made. The lively exchange between the jurors as they moved through the rows of competition boards and the excitement of seeing all the entries displayed simultaneously in a single space created a dynamic environment as jurors discovered the exhilarating, the fantastic, the hilarious, the outrageous, the impossible, the historical, the futuristic, the feasible, the unbelievable, the local, and the obvious.

The winning design, illuminated by thousands of colored light bulbs, was selected for the balance it achieved in creating a mesmerizing project with a direct response and sensitivity to the site. The iconic object not only becomes a destination but also works with the restrictions of a complex site to allow for physical and visual movement through the structure and out to the surrounding landscape. The success of this beautifully crafted architectural landmark lies in a design that respects the historic icon under which it is located but that also has the potential to become an icon itself.

The winning team, Carmody Groarke Hardie, is an emerging group of architects based in London who are on the verge of establishing themselves within the profession. This project exemplifies their integrated approach to design and their willingness to work on a complex process in the hopes of ultimately realizing an eye-catching and memorable symbol of Coney Island's renewal.

An exhibition at the Institute in summer 2005 gave visitors the opportunity to view all 864 entries on an innovative display system designed by Moorhead & Moorhead. A special section was allocated for the winning design, which included a model and animation of the project. This publication builds on the competition and expands its themes with in-depth essays and narratives. While it is clear that design competitions are only a part of a series of steps and decisions that will eventually lead to positive change, our hope is that this volume will expand the discussion and contribute to an international exchange of ideas.

Parachute Pavilion competition jury, 2005

ACKNOWLEDGMENTS

We would like to acknowledge a number of people who made this project possible. Special thanks to former VAI executive director Raymond W. Gastil, CIDC chair Joshua Sirefman, and VAI chair Sherida E. Paulsen for initiating this competition. Many thanks to Brooklyn Borough President Marty Markowitz for his continued support and for contributing an inspiring preface to this book. Our heartfelt thanks to Rem Koolhaas and the Office for Metropolitan Architecture and Andrea Monfried at Monacelli Press for granting us permission to reprint excerpts from *Delirious New York*, Tracy Metz for her lively and informative essay, and Charles Denson for his illuminating historical text and for granting permission to reprint images from his collection. Thanks also to Ludwig Abache, Diana Balmori, Daniel Campo, Sam Casswell, Jake Dobkin, Hollandse Hoogte, Maria Austria Instituut, Herzog and de Meuron, Jason Orton, Bas Princen, Stijn Rolies, UN Studio, Simon Starling, The Royal Collection, Her Majesty Queen Elizabeth II, and Per Gunnar Tverbakk for contributing images to this volume. Our sincere gratitude to Marcus Woollen, competition associate, and Ori Topaz, competition and publication assistant, for their inexhaustible energy and commitment to this project. Thanks to Karen Kice for her sterling design assistance with this book and Jason Rosen for administrative support. This project would not have been possible without the dedication and professionalism of the staff at the EDC, especially Chirag Badlani, Rachel Belskey, Lynn Bodnar, and Kate Collignon. We would also like to recognize the support of the VAI and CIDC board members. Many thanks to Princeton Architectural Press for embracing and supporting this project and publishing this volume. In particular, we would like to acknowledge Kevin Lippert, Clare Jacobson, Linda Lee, and Paul Wagner. Finally we would like to acknowledge all the design teams who inspired us with their entries to the competition.

I. ESSAYS

CONEY ISLAND: A HISTORY OF PAVILIONS
CHARLES DENSON

Alanzo Reed and Thomas Bielby had no idea that they were making history when they opened a primitive dancehall called the Coney Island Pavilion on a lonely, windswept sand dune in the summer of 1845. Although the name Coney Island conjures up kaleidoscopic images of roller coasters, carousels, sideshows, and crowded beaches overflowing with the full spectrum of humanity, the truth is that Coney's magnificence began with the simple structures known as pavilions.

Coney Island's pavilions evolved from its first built structures: open tentlike shelters cobbled together from scraps of sails and driftwood by fishermen and hunters, the island's first visitors. Decades before mechanical amusements and grand spectacles became the island's mainstay, the unspoiled natural environment was Coney's primary attraction. Early engravings portray formally dressed tourists sporting top hats, canes, and parasols watching the antics of clumsy, heavily dressed bathers in the surf. The majority of visitors were cautious beach strollers, not swimmers. This ratio would change as casual observers became outnumbered by active participants.

At first pavilions provided a safe haven for the public to relax and enjoy the natural environment. Soon they also served as changing rooms used by tourists to put on rented woolen swimwear so they could experience the ocean firsthand. Ocean bathing became a revolutionary activity that created a new world of recreation and amusement.

Reed and Bielby's wooden pavilion became Coney Island's first amusement, and by the end of the 1870s, Coney's shorefront was lined with pavilions of every shape and style: dance pavilions, pier pavilions, theatrical pavilions, exhibition pavilions, music pavilions, and picnic pavilions. The elite and exclusive resort establishments at Coney's east end, the Oriental and Manhattan Beach hotels, offered ornate, well-appointed bathing and dining pavilions, while the transient masses visiting the west end patronized modest, barnlike bathhouse pavilions that sprang up around the steam-train terminals.

Coney Island has a long tradition as a resort. Before settlement, the sandbar was used as a summer retreat by the Canarsee Indians. The tribe left great shell mounds along the shore that, in 1823, were excavated and used to pave the first road to the island. It was this road, known as the Shell Road, that opened the island to development.

Shell Road ran from Brooklyn, through the farming village of Gravesend, and south to a bridge and tollhouse at Coney Island Creek. The first visitors were fishermen and "Coney-catchers," the clam diggers whose bounty provided shellfish for the saloons in Manhattan. Later, carriages carrying picnic parties began streaming across the bridge to the beach, even on the Sabbath, which shocked the pious townspeople of Gravesend.

In 1829 the Shell Road's owners constructed a boxy, wood-frame hotel at the road's terminus and named it the Coney Island House. It was a popular and traditional hotel of the era, providing none of the scandalous notoriety that would make Coney the most famous seaside resort in the world.

Coney Island remained formal and relatively peaceful until Bielby and Reed's Coney Island Pavilion opened at the desolate western tip of the island. Consisting of an open, circular wooden dance platform topped with a tent of sails and perched on a tall sand dune, it was accessible only by boat. Reed and Bielby operated daily ferry service from Manhattan to the small dock they built adjacent to their pavilion. The *Brooklyn Eagle* covered the pavilion's opening and recommended a walk along a "long beach of pure sand, where the white caps are continually dancing around and beckoning the timid, as it were, to their healthful embrace." Newspaper advertisements of the day declared the attraction suitable not only for "wives and children," but also for "sportsmen" who were invited to bring their guns along to "hunt sand birds."

Because it was isolated from the snooping towns-people of Gravesend, the Coney Island Pavilion prospered for several decades, even as undesirables caused its reputation to plummet. Gilbert Davis, a dubious character known to locals as the "Governor" of Coney Island, became manager and turned it into the perfect venue for the drunken bacchanals held by political clubs of the Boss Tweed era.

Development of Coney Island began slowly after the Civil War and then exploded during the 1870s as transportation improved. The first steam railroad arrived in 1865, soon followed by four more, each boasting its own landscaped

The Coney Island Pavilion, opened in 1845, was Coney Island's first amusement.

A primitive Civil War–era bathing pavilion provided shade and comfort at Coney Island Point. Reprinted from *Harper's Weekly*, August 17, 1867, 521.

The Brighton Beach Music Pavilion was swept away in a storm in 1884. Chas. F. Schneur, Coney Island, N.Y., Guidebook, 1880.

plazas, hotels, and pavilions at its terminus. Two great iron piers stretching a thousand feet into the ocean offered direct ferry service from Manhattan to the center of the island. Nearby, Olmsted and Vaux's broad promenade called Ocean Parkway, completed in 1876, made travel easier than ever for the carriage trade.

Developers carved Coney Island into four distinct sections. The west end was renamed Norton's Point, for Mike Norton, a crooked New York judge whose fiefdom was headquartered at the Coney Island Pavilion. Corrupt Gravesend political boss John McKane ruled the central area, known as West Brighton. As chief of police, McKane condoned prostitution and gambling, earning Coney the colorful nickname "Sodom by the Sea." Civil War–veteran William Engeman took control of the sand dunes to the east, built a hotel and racetrack, and sold the rest of the property to the developers of Brighton Beach. New York banker Austin Corbin purchased the remote and marshy east end of the island and filled it in to create exclusive Manhattan Beach.

The 1870s proved to be a gold mine not only for big developers but also for the small-time operators who sublet tiny patches of sand for concessions and games. This was the golden age of pavilions. For a decade Coney's beach-front shelters remained the most popular of attractions.

Music pavilions hosted performances by popular military bands of the era, such as John Philip Sousa. Bathing pavilions provided locker rooms, towels, and showers for beachgoers. Restaurant pavilions boasted open-air dining featuring sumptuous seafood feasts known as "shore dinners." The massive pavilions atop the Iron Piers allowed patrons to promenade or waltz high above the crashing waves. Rest pavilions provided weary visitors with a shady place to sit, relax, and enjoy ocean breezes. Oddly shaped amusement pavilions, topped with onion domes and colorful flags, housed all types of fun machines. Every beachfront hotel had a "summer pavilion" with verandas at the water's edge, a place for patrons to escape the rain or scorching sun.

Some of the pavilions were less than elaborate. Along the alley known as the Bowery, open taverns like Solomon Perry's Glass Pavilion and the Elephant Pavilion beckoned strollers inside to quench their thirst. Lining the beach were tiny ramshackle "clam pavilions" made from wrecked vessels that washed up in the surf.

An 1874 *Atlantic Monthly* article described the old Norton & Murray's Pavilion as a "large, windy frame building that has weathered the storms of the coast for many a year. Every pore in its planks, every joint, every crack, is thoroughly saturated with sand. Sand, instead of

pepper, appears to have been used in the compilation of its clam chowders and oyster stews, and it is here, of all places, that the sandwich appears to be most truthfully denoted by its time-honored name."

In contrast was Corbin's luxurious Manhattan Beach Pavilion, which seated nearly 2,000 guests and served more than 5,000 meals per day. It also housed a bandstand, an amphitheater, and 3,200 bathhouses, described as being "constructed of the best hardwood, tastefully painted inside and out, and supplied with running water and gas."

Engeman's Brighton Bathing Pavilion, while not as fashionable as Corbin's, was probably the largest on the island—a sprawling, block-long, four-story structure, capped with a domed tower. Charles Feltman, the German immigrant credited with inventing the hot dog, built his Ocean Pavilion in 1876 and later expanded it to include carousels, an outdoor movie theater, a restaurant, and a Tyrolean village with costumed singing waiters. Coney's two most elegant pavilions were a rustic, heavy-timbered pair located on the Concourse at the foot of Ocean Parkway.

Then there was the grandest pavilion of all: the Sea Beach Palace. The palace started out as the United States Government Pavilion at the Philadelphia Centennial and in 1877 was transported by barge to Coney Island and reassembled on the beach. It served as a restaurant, hotel, and terminal for the Sea Beach Railroad before being converted to a roller rink.

In 1884 the world's first roller coaster was built at Coney; a hotel in the shape of a colossal elephant opened shortly after. The stage was set for the fantastic and unusual attractions that would make the island world famous. In the coming decades, as mechanical amusements became the big draw, Coney's natural environment would be lost. The ocean could no longer be reached without pay-ing a bathhouse fee, and encroachment reduced the beach to a mere sliver that disappeared altogether at high tide.

The period from 1895 to 1910 was Coney's heyday, a time when millions flocked to the island. Three fantastic amusement parks coexisted with grand hotels, racetracks, and theaters. The Iron Tower, rising three hundred feet above the beach, was New York's tallest structure and was visible from fifty miles out at sea. Coney's first amuse-ment park, Sea Lion Park, opened in 1895, followed by Steeplechase Park in 1897, Luna in 1903, and Dreamland in 1904.

After a disastrous fire destroyed Steeplechase Park in 1907, founder George C. Tilyou built what would become Coney's most famous pavilion: the Steeplechase Pavilion of

Japanese tea pavilions at Luna Park provided an exotic touch, 1903.

William Engeman's bathing pavilion at Brighton Beach was Coney's largest. Reprinted from Chas. F. Schneur, *Coney Island, N.Y., Guidebook*, 1881.

Makeshift pavilions lined Coney Island's beach in 1878. Reprinted from *Harper's Weekly*, August 3, 1878, 632.

Rustic pavilions greeted visitors at the terminus of Ocean Parkway in 1877. Reprinted from *Harper's Weekly*, August 4, 1877, 604.

At dusk, the crystalline towers of Dreamland were illuminated by thousands of light bulbs, ca. 1906.

When viewed from inside, the Steeplechase Pavilion of Fun's painted facade glowed like stained glass, ca. 1960.

Rest pavilions were a welcome feature of the new boardwalk when it opened in 1923.

The sweeping steel trusses and ornate columns of the Steeplechase Pavilion of Fun created a visual delight, 1908.

Weber's Carousel Pavilion was located on the boardwalk at West Twenty-seventh Street, 1940s.

The Steeplechase Pavilion was demolished before it could gain landmark status.

Fun. Standing seven stories tall and covering nearly three acres, the Steeplechase pavilion was a steel-and-glass "fun factory" based on an industrial design. The building solved one of Coney's inherent problems: inclement weather. Whenever the island's outdoor amusements were rained out, the indoor pavilion remained open to thousands of patrons who sought shelter, welcoming them with a variety of rides, restaurants, concessions, a ballroom, games, and live shows.

During World War I, the city began a successful effort to reclaim the beaches from private developers. In 1923 a boardwalk was built over a new beach created with sand pumped from offshore. Featured on the new boardwalk were six beautiful Mediterranean-style pavilions. The public would enjoy these beachfront "rest pavilions" for the next fifty years. In the late 1920s, one last great pavilion opened at Coney Island, Weber's Carousel Pavilion, a glass-shed structure designed by the same architect responsible for the Steeplechase Pavilion of Fun.

Coney remained a popular destination through the Great Depression and World War II, before entering a long decline hastened by Parks Commissioner Robert Moses, who declared the area a redevelopment zone in 1949. Weber's Carousel Pavilion was demolished in 1957, and the boardwalk pavilions succumbed to arson, burning during the 1970s.

The most heartbreaking loss was the demolition of the Steeplechase pavilion in 1966 by developer Fred Trump, who destroyed the structure before it could be landmarked. Trump had sought a zoning change that was never granted, and the city later reclaimed the property and converted it into a park. Until recently, the only reminder of Coney's golden age of pavilions was a small, crumbling concrete shelter on the boardwalk near the aquarium. In 2000 Coney's fortunes changed when a new ballpark, subway terminal, and boardwalk pavilion were built. Then, in 2005, the Parachute Pavilion was proposed, launching a bright new chapter in Coney's history.

Charles Denson is the author of *Coney Island: Lost and Found* (Ten Speed Press, 2002) and is the executive director of the Coney Island History Project, a nonprofit oral history organization dedicated to preserving Coney Island in living memory.

Coney Island: The Technology of the Fantastic

"The glare is everywhere, and nowhere a shadow."
—Maxim Gorky, "Boredom"

"What a sight the poor make in the moonlight."
—James Huneker, *The New Cosmopolis*

"Hell is very badly done."
—Maxim Gorky, "Boredom"

*   *   *

Model

Now, where the waste was…rise to the sky a thousand glittering towers and minarets, graceful, stately, and imposing. The morning sun looks down on these as it might upon the magically realized dream of a poet or painter.

At night, the radiance of the millions of electric lights which glow at every point and life and curve of the great play city's outlines lights up the sky and welcomes the home coming mariner thirty miles from the shore.

Or:

With the advent of night a fantastic city of fire suddenly rises from the ocean into the sky. Thousands of ruddy sparks glimmer in the darkness, limning in fine, sensitive outline on the black background of the sky shapely towers of miraculous castles, palaces, and temples.

Golden gossamer threads tremble in the air. They intertwine in transparent flaming patterns, which flutter and melt away, in love with their own beauty mirrored in the waters.

Fabulous beyond conceiving, ineffably beautiful, is this fiery scintillation. Coney Island around 1905: it is no coincidence that the countless "impressions of Coney Island"—products of a hopelessly obstinate desire to record and preserve a mirage—can all be substituted not only for each other but also for the flood of later descriptions of Manhattan. At the junction of the 19th and 20th centuries, Coney Island is the incubator for Manhattan's incipient themes and infant mythology. The strategies and mechanisms that later shape Manhattan are tested in the laboratory of Coney Island before they finally leap toward the larger island.

Coney Island is a fetal Manhattan.

*   *   *

Electricity

Similar adaptations follow at a constantly accelerating rate.

The inordinate number of people assembling on the inadequate acreage, ostensibly seeking confrontation with the reality of the elements (sun, wind, sand, water) *demands* the systematic conversion of nature into a technical service.

Since the total surface area of the beach and the total length of surf line are finite, it follows with mathematical certainty that the hundreds of thousands of visitors will not each find a place to spread out on the sand, let alone reach the water, within a single day.

Toward 1890, the introduction of electricity makes it possible to create a second daytime. Bright lights are placed at regular intervals along the surf line, so that now the sea can be enjoyed on a truly metropolitan shift-system, giving those unable to reach the water in the daytime a man-made 12-hour extension.

What is unique in Coney Island—and this syndrome of the Irresistible Synthetic prefigures later events in Manhattan—is that this false daytime is not regarded as second-rate.

Its very artificiality becomes an attraction: "Electric Bathing."

* * *

Astronauts

In 1903, the year the new Williamsburg Bridge injects even more visitors into Coney Island's already overtaxed system, Frederic Thompson and Elmer Dundy open a second park—Luna.

Thompson doubles the isolation of Luna Park by imposing a theme that embraces the entire site in a system of metaphorical meaning: its surface is to be "not of this earth" but part of the Moon. On entering Luna Park's masses are turned into astronauts in a conceptual airlock through which they all have to pass.

* * *

Theory

Thompson has created the first City of Towers: functionless, except to overstimulate the imagination and keep any recognizable earthly realities at a distance. Now he uses electricity—the essential ingredient of the new paraphernalia of illusion—as an architectural duplicator.

In broad daylight, Luna's small towers have a pathetic dimension, an aura of cheapness, but by superimposing over its skyline a network of wires and light bulbs, Thompson described a second, illusory skyline, even more impressive than the first, a separate *city of night*.

"In the wilderness of the sky and ocean rises the magic picture of a flaming city" and "with the advent of night a fantastic city all of fire suddenly rises from the ocean into the sky…Fabulous beyond conceiving, ineffably beautiful, is this fiery scintillation."

For the price of one, Thompson has created two distinct cities, each with its own character, its own life, and its own inhabitants. Now the city *itself* is to be lived in shifts; the electric city, phantom offspring of the "real" city, is an even more powerful instrument for the fulfillment of fantasy.

CALCULATING LEISURE
TRACY METZ

Since the days of Dutch photographer Carel Blazer's pictures of merry-go-rounds taken in the 1950s, leisure and recreation have, you might say, grown up. They have become more commercial. More calculated. More designed, less authentic. More formalized, less coincidental. A means to an end rather than an end in itself. City planners, politicians, and designers use leisure as a tool for place making and even as a motor for urban regeneration. Where housing was once held to be the most important program for new land use or the rehabilitation of disused areas, leisure functions and spaces have now become at least as essential a part of any grand urban design.

In the regeneration of former harbor areas, everywhere from Hamburg to Montreal, Amsterdam to Barcelona, Copenhagen to Genoa, fun is employed as a strategy for bringing in crowds, liveliness, and income. A competition the Netherlands-based architecture firm UN Studio won in Genoa, Italy, is a case in point: in the Porto Antico adjacent to the city center, Ben van Berkel's office is restructuring the 900,000 square feet of the old pier of Ponte Parodi into "a three-dimensional piazza." A sculptured roof, explains project architect Nuno Almeida, accommodates retail establishments, restaurants, a concert hall, and a small cruise terminal at ground level and creates sports areas, gardens, and a beach-related program with sand, water, and events above. "The pier is big, but still too small for a major attractor like the Imax theater or the shopping center in Barcelona," says Almeida. "The emphasis here is not so much on the building itself as on the integration of public and commercial spaces."[1]

Undeniably, leisure can bring spaces back into the public realm that were previously inaccessible and that had become white spots on the city map. An example is the miracle Germany has wrought in the Ruhrgebiet, for decades a soot-bedecked industrial area full of coal mines, gas holders, and chemical factories. Now it has been refurbished and opened to the public to use as parks, climbing walls, diving schools, open-air cinemas, museums, and theaters. Copenhagen celebrated the clean up of the river by mooring a large, sculptural wooden platform to the bank with deep and shallow pools, a diving tower, a sunbathing area, and a little kiosk for basic food and drink. It is immensely popular in summertime, and not only because it is free.

Everywhere waterfront communities are being reconceived and new public spaces are emerging—but there is a flip side. To a hitherto unknown extent, these spaces are interwoven with private, or commercial, interests and are exploited by local politicians as marketing instruments. There is now almost always an agenda, an ulterior motive to leisure space, be it commercial or political. New York's preservationists managed to rescue South Street Seaport from demolition when the fish market closed—that is to say, the structure has been preserved, but the place has been "Rousefied"—commoditized into a so-called festival marketplace by developer Rouse, with stylish restaurants and cute shops catering entirely to tourists. No more slimy guts and fish scales on the picturesque cobblestones, please!

Tits & Ass

The phenomenon of the topless beach has always intrigued me, and not just because of what there is to see. What intrigues me is the spatial code. The topless beach can only exist thanks to a widely recognized social covenant that reads as follows: *here* you are in the normal world and therefore are deemed to wear at least a modicum of body cover; *there*, on the other side of an invisible line in the sand, you are free to show all (or most), even though you may be surrounded by many more people *there* than *here*.

Going topless is of course an extreme form of the vagaries of dress codes, but more interestingly, it says something about the *status aparte* of the seafront and the power of place that the waterside exerts in general. It imparts a sense of liberation. The best proof of this I can remember is a trip I took to the beach with the boy next door and his family when we were growing up in Los Angeles. His father had always struck me as quite an ordinary guy, but in the car the man revealed a whole new side of himself. To my amazement, and his wife's chagrin, he started humming, then singing his own lyrics to the tune of the rollicking John Philip Sousa march: "Tits & ass tits & ass tits & ass-ass-ass, tits & ass…." You get the idea. It was obvious what the attractions of a day at the beach were for him.

At the same time, another powerful image comes to mind when I think about the lure of the waterfront. It is a photograph taken by Carel Blazer in 1953, presumably at

Fairground Muiderberg, Holland, 1953

Aerial view of Porto Antico, Genoa, Italy, 2001

Rendering of UN Studio's proposal for transforming a former pier into a piazza sul mediterraneo (a square on the water), at Porto Antico, Genoa, Italy, 2001

Left to right: South Street Seaport, New York,
New York, 2006

a traveling village fair on the coast of the Ijsselmeer, the Netherlands. A merry-go-round with swings stands at the edge of the water; in the distance we see people wading. All but one of the swings are empty, emphasizing the summer feeling that we all remember from childhood, when time hangs suspended, interrupted perhaps only by the boy's shriek as he whirls around. A nostalgic image, innocent, reminiscent of a time when fun had no hidden agenda and had not yet been shanghaid into the service of urban designers and image builders.

Fun in the sun: it must be one of mankind's oldest and most basic forms of recreation. But in the past ten or fifteen years, we have witnessed a fundamental transformation of recreation and leisure. We spend more and more energy and more and more money on our free time—and at least as much if not more on its accoutrements. I think it's safe to say that many more of us spend a lot more time browsing at the adventure store REI than we do ice-climbing or rafting; more of us nose around a Niketown than work up a sweat on the basketball court. We think we're shopping for the attributes we need for the pursuit of leisure activities, but shopping is a leisure activity in its own right. It is a vicarious form of participation in the theme at hand, *in casu* (outdoor) sports.

The way we dress expresses the importance we attach to the sporty and the casual as an expression of a desirable look and lifestyle. Even if we're not in the least athletic, we wear high-tech Michael Jordan sneakers to McDonald's. We may have no time or inclination to go hiking and camping, but that doesn't stop us from wearing Goretex hiking boots and fleece jackets and schlepping our books and papers and laptop back and forth to class or to the office in backpacks rugged enough for an ascent of the Himalayas.

In the northwestern United States, we can see an example of how shopping and outdoor sports come together to create new places and new destinations. This is where Cabela's has set up business, huge emporia filled with every conceivable piece of equipment the hunter and the angler could possibly need, in a breathtaking decor of dozens of stuffed trophies arranged in realistic poses on a faux mountain. Cabela's works on the same principle as a casino, holding onto customers for as long as possible by offering not only sports goods but also furniture (glass lamps and coffee tables with stuffed quail inside), a restaurant (all the fried chicken you can eat for a couple of dollars), an aquarium, a shooting gallery, and racks of picture postcards (proof that it is a tourist destination). Along with the Cabela's big-box stores, hotel chains and gas stations open up and even warrant their own separate

freeway entrance and exit. Leisure not only uses existing places, it generates new ones.

The strong grip that leisure has on our imagination has permeated not just the way we look and the way we spend our time and money, but also the way we utilize space and the nature of these new places we make. A fascinating example of a brand-new, totally leisure-driven waterfront landscape is the immense new development off the coast of Dubai, the United Arab Emirates. Consortia from all over the world have been brought in to make artificial islands in the shape of palm trees and archipelagos, representing a miniature version of "the world." Here, the world's wealthy can buy a villa as a part-time residence and shop in the megamall complete with ski slope. The yacht industry is expecting a big boost from the development of Dubai, and the entire Middle East is feeling the shortage of building cranes as Dubai soaks up all the available resources.

Sand on asphalt

Such is the power of the waterfront as a mental concept, as a place we long for, that it has spawned a whole spate of urban "beaches." Fun in the sun and sand in the city without even having to go out of town. Europe's first urban beach was in Paris, where, in 2001, the event's organizer Jean-Christophe Choblet came up with the idea of closing off the Seine to vehicular traffic, dumping truckloads of sand along the street, wheeling in rows of potted palms and parasols, and declaring it Paris Plage. It was a wild success, no doubt thanks to the many Parisiennes who obligingly arranged themselves in bikinis along the retaining walls, adding a novel urban touch to the age-old beach agenda of tits & ass. The example was set: Vienna, Brussels, Berlin, Budapest, Rome, Rotterdam all followed suit. You can even set a theme for an urban beach: in the summer of 2005, parts of Paris Plage were dubbed "Ipanema" and "Copacabana," with concerts of Brazilian music, beach soccer, and a samba school.

Amsterdam's first urban beach even went so far as to do without sand altogether: on the tilting roof of Renzo Piano's science museum, the organizers set out rows of green bean bags and served Bacardi Breezers—it now charges an admission fee of two and half euros—and all of hip Amsterdam came flocking. The fact that the roof slopes toward the city, and not toward the water on the other side of the museum, did not cause objections. The urban beaches in Berlin were particularly interesting: they sprang up out of the German capital's underground scene, and at first appeared, guerrillalike, in the courtyards of buildings slated for demolition. The municipal authorities were initially worried, but relaxed when they realized that the beaches were bringing life to parts of town that needed a social boost—a boost for which the government might otherwise have had to foot the bill.

Artificial beaches obviously hold commercial promise but realizing that promise is a whole different thing. A Singaporean businessman and a Malaysian investment company poured seventy million euros into the Tropical Islands Resort, which opened in early 2004 in a hangar destined for an airship located between Berlin and Dresden in Brandenburg, the province with the highest unemployment of all of former East Germany. The locals, of course, hope it will bring in tourist euros, but so far it is slightly crepuscular in the hangar's 66,000 square meters, and the palm trees are fighting for their lives.

It can get even weirder. Japan built an artificial beach on Miyazaki, the southernmost Kyushu Island, with a vault over it that can move back and forth depending on the weather. Every aspect is controlled in a way that evokes both the Forum shops in Las Vegas' Caesar Palace, where the sun rises and sets every hour, and the movie set of *The Truman Show*. Perhaps the most bizarre thing about this beach theme park is that it is actually at the beach—but the real beach is empty, as visitors prefer the predictability, safety, and cleanliness of the man-made environment. The water doesn't sting your eyes because it's not salty, every hour the "volcano" erupts, the computer creates the perfect surfing waves, and it is always a balmy 86 degrees, every day of the year. Ron Gluckman, the Hong Kong–based American journalist, blogs:

> Paradise proceeds with clockwork precision inside Ocean Dome, Japan's unique, sometimes surrealistic, but utterly updated version of the Garden of Eden. In Ocean Dome, once every hour, on the hour, the surf is always up. Every afternoon is a carnival. Mechanized parrots squawk from branches of the dome's ingenious rain forest, which remain lush and tropical without rainfall or humidity. Best of all, in Ocean Dome, you can lull for hours on crushed marble pebbles without a worry about beach vendors, bugs or sun burns.[2]

The beach has been liberated from the physical constraints of the actual coast: a beach can be anywhere, as long as we all accept the illusion. Sand on asphalt or concrete is still sand, isn't it?

The banks of the River Seine converted into an urban beach, Paris Plage, 2003

Ocean Dome, Miyazaki, Japan, 1998

End of the Highway, 2001. A Peugeot car owners' club has picked the barren industrial Maasvlakte, a man-made addition to the industrial harbor area near Rotterdam, the Netherlands, as its gathering place.

Car beach, 2001. Kite flying on the Maasvlakte.

Monumental dereliction

All these self-conscious, hyper-designed, business-modeled recreational opportunities make some people thirst for the opposite: informal, unorganized, rough-and-tumble recreation in places that were never intended to serve as leisure venues. Let's call them cranky statements of anticommodification, where a whiff of danger (pollution, scrap iron with sharp edges, derelict buildings) only serves to heighten the thrill.

Rotterdam has such a place: the Maasvlakte, designed as an expansion for the harbor. It is a man-made environment, thoroughly rational and industrial, nothing cute or romantic about it. The Maasvlakte has been adopted by groups of people looking for recreation without a concept, an unprogrammed space where they can do whatever it is they want to do: watching the seals on the sand banks, sunbathing, picnicking, flying kites, surfing. Recreation on the Maasvlakte is in its own way a lifestyle statement.

Brooklyn has such a place too: the Brooklyn Eastern District Terminal (BEDT), a twenty-acre rail-marine transhipment facility vacated in 1983. Daniel Campo, currently a lecturer at the Department of Community and Regional Planning at Temple University, wrote his dissertation on this "vernacular" recreation:

With the Midtown Manhattan skyline as its backdrop, BEDT's collapsing piers, eroded bulkhead, remaining building foundations, construction debris and dumped objects became the raw materials for various forms of waterfront recreation. These vernacular uses include everything from simple things like fishing or bird watching to more organized events such as art shows, performances, film shoots, concerts, but also a skatepark and homeless encampments.[3]

For these various groups of users, he has coined the new term "recreational constituencies." His pictures show people barbecuing, sunbathing, skating, and just plain hanging out in a landscape of weeds, junk, and broken pieces of concrete. Obviously, there the incomplete, the abandoned, the serendipitous exert a strong pull, also as leisure venues. Campo is convinced that the unplanned character of the abandoned terminal and the informal use Brooklynites make of it are essential to urban culture, but he sees dark clouds on the horizon: "Those sites that support the greatest amount and the widest variety of uses are also those that are most desirable to developers and the various city agencies that preside over development."[4]

Informal, or "vernacular," recreation at the Brooklyn Eastern District Terminal (BEDT), a twenty-acre rail-marine transshipment facility vacated in 1983, 2001. Unplanned multiuse leisure spaces like these are essential to urban culture, and they are also very attractive for developers and city authorities.

He believes they warrant a more formalized recognition and perhaps a "mechanism" to protect them from conventional development. Ultimately, though, Campo comes to the wistful conclusion that bringing these spaces under the umbrella of established political order would probably destroy much of the "other" qualities that make these spaces so compelling in the first place." Indeed, Brooklyn has started rezoning this former industrial area for residential use with the inevitable esplanade.

All the paradoxes and delicious ironies of leisure, recreation, tourism, preservation, and urban regeneration come together in an out-of-the-way place: the deserted town of Nyksund, above the polar circle in Norway. Nyksund was traditionally a fishing village, with a handsome waterfront of two-story wooden houses built on stilts to accommodate the tides. Decline set in, however, as the fishing fleet was modernized: ships got bigger and Nyksund's harbor was too small. In the seventies, government decided to buy the inhabitants out and move them to a town 18.5 miles away; the houses were left to weather and grow into ruins.

In the eighties, however, Nyksund underwent an unexpected revival. First a group of German junkies on a detox program started rebuilding the houses. As word spread, the village was rediscovered by outdoors types and by artists with a sensibility for the aesthetics of decay. Moreover, since government had essentially given it up, there were no rules and regulations. This status of a free haven gave it a special allure in Norway's highly regulated society. Nyksund now has six to eight permanent residents in the winter and hundreds in the summer. Now, however, the municipality's policy of gradual decline is biting itself in the tail: the very people who like Nyksund because it is off the beaten path are pressuring local government to invest again in the road that leads to it. (No fish guts on the cobblestones of South Street Seaport, please, and no potholes in the road to a romantic ruin!)

In the nineties, Norway's Arts Council started the project Artscape Nordland. One of the artists involved was the Scotsman and Turner Prize–winner Simon Starling. Surveying the range of projects completed before him, he explains by email: "I was struck by their general sense of solidity and permanence. They somehow attempt to defy their very location, to resist its power."[5] His contribution was to be very different. In 2004 he proposed taking the last quayside wooden house—which by now is decayed to the point that it resembles wooden lace—and setting it afloat on a pontoon in the bay, like a folly, and transported by sea to other locations. A mobile ruin, a nomadic monument.

Simon Starling, "Floating Folly," art proposal (photomontage) for Nyksund, Norway, 2004.

Having seen a picture of the floating folly, I blithely assumed that the project existed. No. It has yet to be realized and may never be. Nyksund has been refurbished to the point that there is only one of the original derelict fisherman's houses left. It was this one that Starling had in mind, and there is a general feeling of reluctance about uprooting it and setting it afloat. How ironic, I thought, and how fitting.

It reminded me of another poignant remark Starling made about the transformation of Nyksund: "The gradual refurbishment of the buildings and infrastructure could be seen as a kind of creeping loss, for with the 'gentrification' of Nyksund comes a kind of historical amnesia." This could be applied to New York's Coney Island too. The wooden roller coaster on Coney Island (Coney = *konijn*, the Dutch word for rabbit), a mere hundred yards from the sea, was for many years one of the twentieth century's most imposing ruins. Coney Island has acquired new fame as an icon of fun fallen on hard times. If Coney Island is Athens, the roller coaster is the Acropolis. That has value in itself, for a good ruin is hard to come by. The competition for the new Parachute Pavilion is the telltale sign that those days are drawing to an end and Coney Island is set for a new lease on life.

Notes

1 Nuno Almeida, in discussion with author, January 2006.

2 Ron Gluckman, "The Great Indoors: Sun, Sand and Surf Were Everyone's Prescription for Holiday Paradise, but, in the South of Japan, They Leave Nothing to Mother Nature," Ron Gluckman in Cyberspace, http://www.gluckman.com/IndoorBeach.html.

3 Daniel Campo, "On the Waterfront: Vernacular Recreation at Brooklyn Eastern District Terminal" (PhD diss., University of Pennsylvania, 2004).

4 ——, "Brooklyn's Vernacular Waterfront," *Journal of Urban Design* 7–2 (2002).

5 Simon Starling, email message to author, January 2006.

Tracy Metz, a native of California, is a journalist with Holland's daily newspaper *NRC Handelsblad*, for which she writes about architecture, landscape, and urban design. She is also an international correspondent for *Architectural Record* and a Loeb Fellow at Harvard University during the 2006–7 academic year. She has collaborated with photographers on a number of books, published by the Netherlands Architecture Institute, including *FUN! Leisure and Landscape* (2002).

II. WINNING DESIGNS

CARMODY GROARKE HARDIE: KEVIN CARMODY, ANDREW GROARKE, CHRIS HARDIE, LEWIS KINNEIR / LONDON, UNITED KINGDOM

This project, an illuminated glass pavilion covered in a matrix of light bulbs, floats above the Coney Island promenade, next to the landmark Parachute Jump. The interior of a singular stepped space is left open to house a gallery, restaurant, and/or beach shop. The unusual abstract form of the pavilion stands as a new landmark for Coney Island and pays homage to its iconic neighbor. The surfaces of the pavilion—floors, walls, and ceilings—are perforated with voids and windows that are deliberately aligned to frame views of the Parachute Jump and the ocean.

By raising the pavilion above the boardwalk, visitors are able to walk freely around the structure and directly across the site twenty-four hours a day via a ramped public space underneath the cantilevered form. The project responds to the overall master plan for the area by fostering connectivity between the boardwalk and Surf Avenue. The overhanging section of the pavilion provides shade from the sun and shelter during the winter. It is punctuated by a single shaft of daylight that penetrates the structure through a cut-out window, marking the entrance while at the same time polarizing views of the Parachute Jump.

The building is made from materials that relate strongly to its context—the boardwalk, the colors of the beachfront, and the lights of Coney Island. A diagonal grid of light bulbs wraps the elevated pavilion, protected by a layer of highly colored glass. The lights dematerialize the form: the pavilion appears to defy gravity. The decorative effect of color and pattern reminds us that this design could only be situated among the fairground structures of Coney Island.

Team Profile

Kevin Carmody, Andrew Groarke, and Chris Hardie met at the London office of David Chipperfield Architects, where they completed several award-winning and widely published projects in the United Kingdom, Europe, and the United States.

Since 2003 Carmody and Groarke have been working together on projects in the United Kingdom and Australia. They have collaborated with Hardie on several independent projects and were recently awarded first place for the 2004 open international Chicago Burnham Prize Competition. Lewis Kinneir began collaborating with the team in 2005.

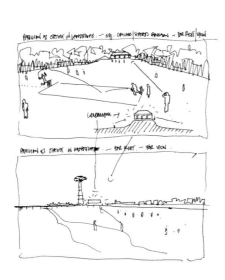

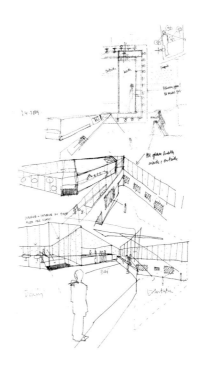

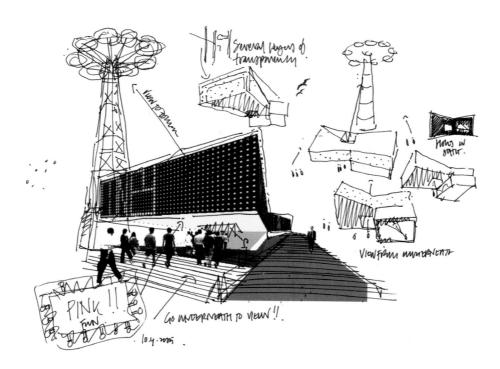

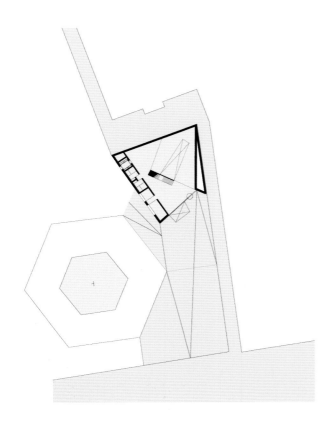

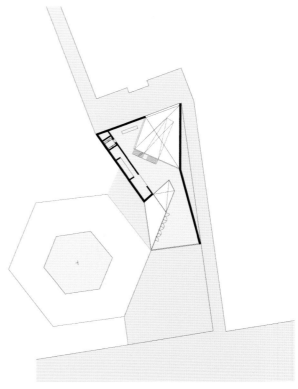

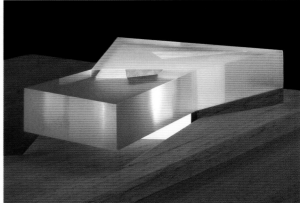

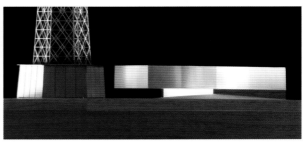

Inspired by the contours, material and color of the jump, the second-place winners, Bateman Architecture, led by Rotterdam-based Ramon Knoester and Brooklyn-based Eckart Graeve, have created a modern addition that creates a balanced ensemble of the historical and the new. The design for the Parachute Pavilion is a tribute to the iconic Parachute Jump but also a whimsical reorganization of the original design.

By sinking the exhibition space below the ground, the roof creates an access to the boardwalk. The pavilion is perforated with round windows that allow the public to peek inside from three sides of the boardwalk. Directly connected to the exhibition space is the store, a visually open volume encircled by canopies that provide shade in warm weather. The restaurant is envisioned as an all-season attraction located on top of the store, with a panoramic view across the boardwalk and beach. A terrace on the roof is designed as an open-air lounge with seating and a reflecting pool. Both the restaurant and terrace is accessed by circular elevators that add the thrill of a ride to this exciting structure.

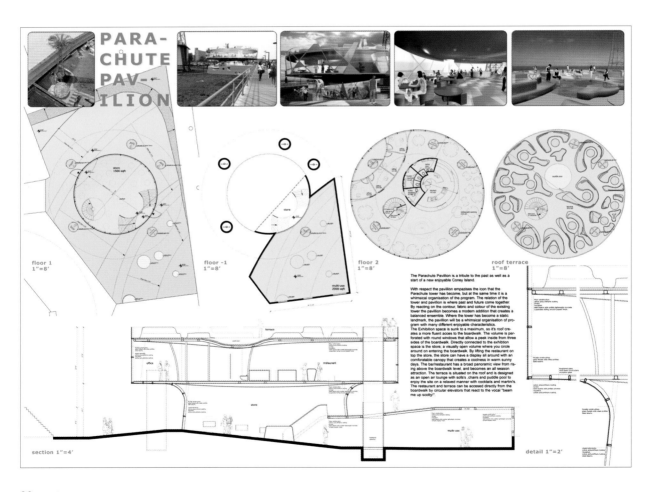

Above, beneath, between, in front, inside—the project by Roman Torres, Patrick Stinger, Mayva Marshall, and Adam Montalbano of 20/2 Collaborative takes the boardwalk as the key theme, locating spaces for exhibitions, a restaurant, a store, and a tourist office within its frame. The stepped extension of the boardwalk climbs up to become the roof of the pavilion, then wraps down and splits apart to enclose the core public spaces inside. One more turn and the boardwalk becomes the floor again and rejoins the beachfront. With these wraps and turns, the boundary between the building and the public space is blurred, enlivening the spectacle of the boardwalk.

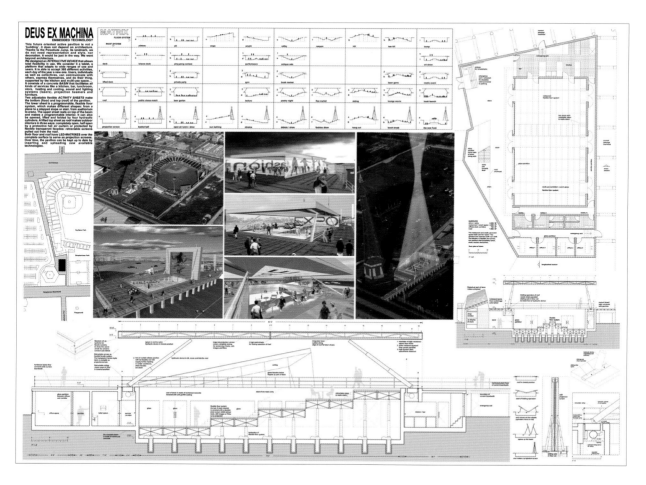

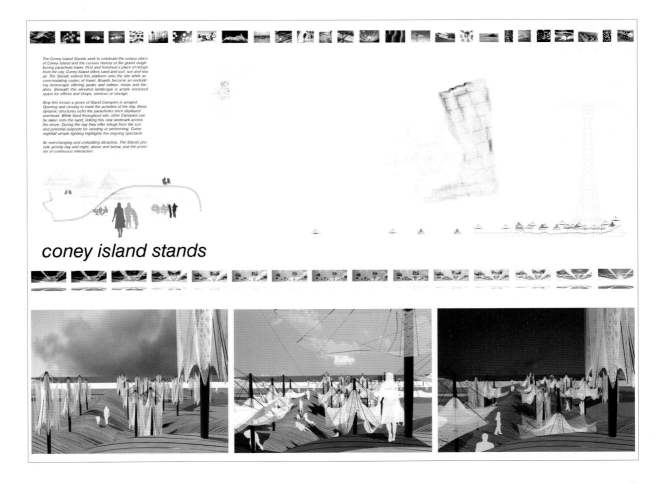

The Coney Island Stands seek to celebrate the unique place of Coney Island and the curious history of the grand neighboring parachute tower. First and foremost a place of refuge from the city, Coney Island offers sand and surf, sun and sea air. The Stands extend this platform onto the site while accommodating routes of travel. Boards become an undulating dunescape offering peaks and valleys, vistas and theaters. Beneath this elevated landscape is ample enclosed space for offices and shops, services or storage.

Atop this terrain a grove of Stand Canopies is arrayed. Opening and closing to meet the activities of the day, these dynamic structures echo the parachutes once deployed overhead. While fixed throughout site, other Canopies can be taken onto the sand, linking this new landmark across the shore. During the day they offer refuge from the sun and potential outposts for vending or performing. Come nightfall simple lighting highlights the ongoing spectacle.

An everchanging and undulating attraction, The Stands provide activity day and night, above and below, and the promise of continuous interaction.

coney island stands

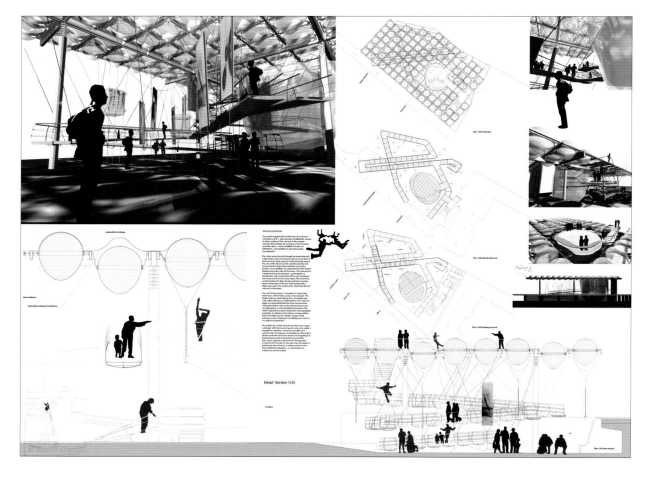

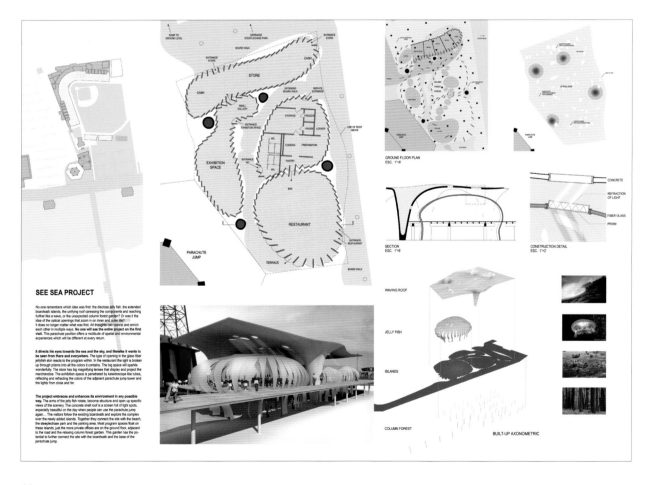

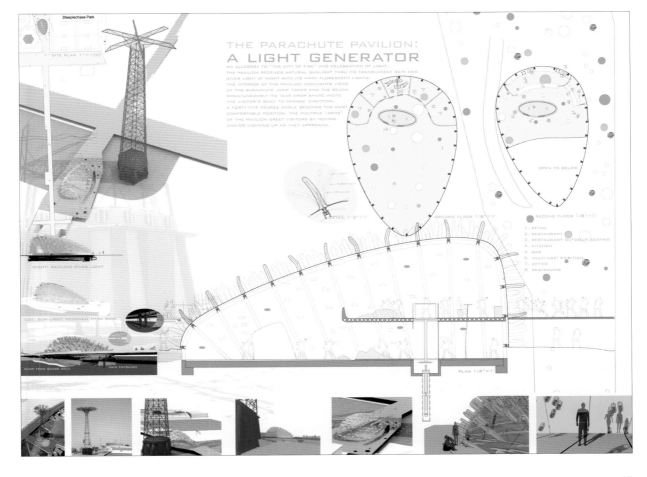

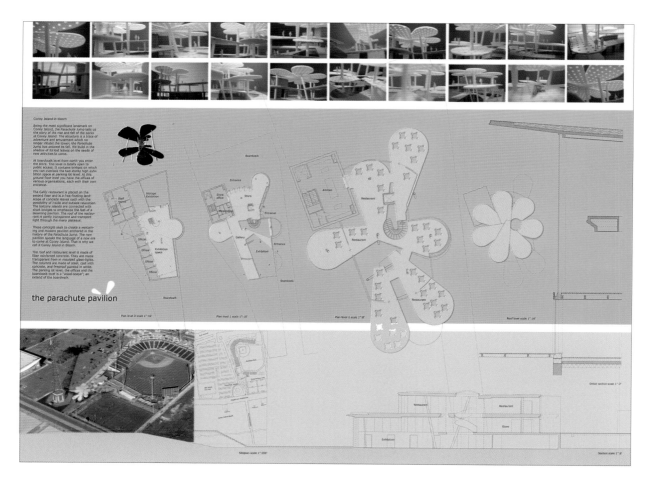

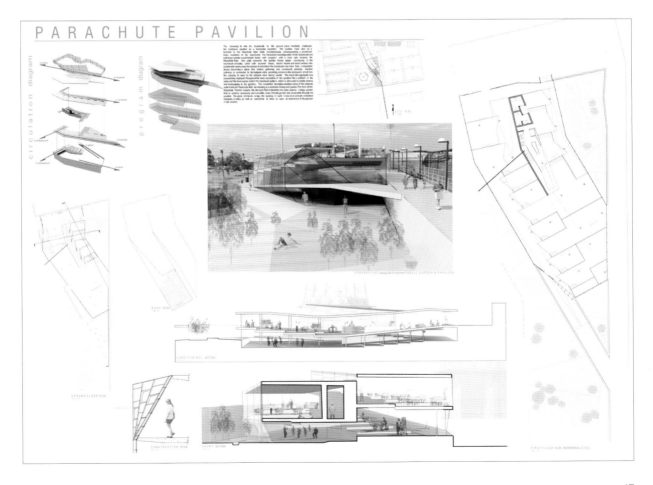

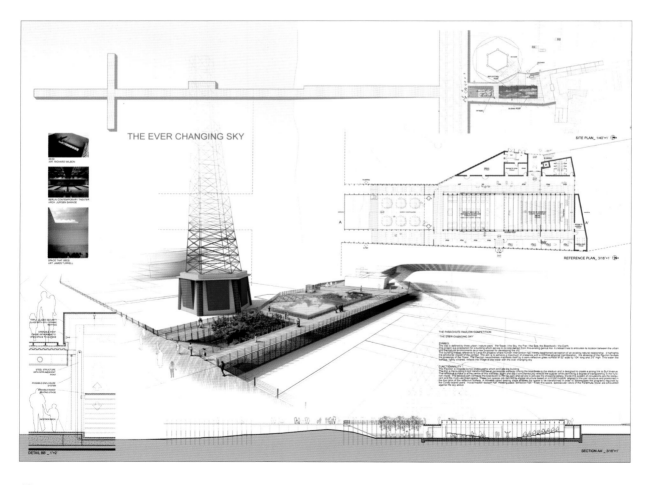

THE EVER CHANGING SKY

III. SELECTED PROJECTS

The following projects are highlighted as particularly inventive submissions to The Parachute Pavilion Competition. They are divided into ten themes: **(IN)SUSPENSE**, **BEACHSCAPE**, **TACTILE TECH-STYLE**, **CONEYSCOPE**, **EXTENDING THE BOARDWALK**, **BEYOND THE BRIEF**, **ARCHI-TYPE**, **ACTIVE (S)PACE**, **MEDIUM AS MEDIA**, and **TAKE AWAY**. These groupings reveal thought-provoking juxtapositions and illustrate the diversity of the submissions. The extraordinary response to The Parachute Pavilion Competition, the largest in the Institute's one-hundred-year history of design competitions, and the high caliber of the projects demonstrates the critical role of design and architecture in the regeneration of cities and the importance of recreation in elevating the quality of public life.

(IN)SUSPENSE

Either physically suspended or providing a sensation of suspense, these dynamic projects float, jump, levitate, peel, and hang—keeping the user in suspense. Some are a direct reference to Coney Island's history, playing tribute to the thrill of the Parachute Jump. Others project a vision of future recreational activities at Coney Island.

Jose Minguell, Laura McQuary (San Antonio, Texas)

PARACHUTE PAVILION

PLAZA / LOWER LEVEL

BOARDWALK LEVEL VIEW

SECTION THROUGH PLAZA

PROJECTION VIEWING AREA

BOARDWALK LEVEL

BIRDS EYE VIEW

SITE PLAN

This Parachute Pavilion celebrates the identity of the Tower and the liveliness of the Boardwalk. Its minimal elements create a communal landscape that invites one to inhabit or simply transverse the spaces. The horizontality of the pavilion resonates with the verticality of the Tower. Likewise, a circular opening in the Pavilion roof frames the view of the tower for pedestrians passing along the Boardwalk. Set within this cutout an engineered transparent glass: streaming digital images about the Tower's history or events are projected on top of the framed tower view. The pavilion roof, made of wood planks, acts as an extension of the Boardwalk. The walkable surface of the Pavilion's peeled back roof creates a small plaza where people can congregate. The tunnel links this plaza with a sheltered terrace on the Beach-facing side of the pavilion and the pier beyond. This tunnel, plaza and terrace also set up the potential venue for larger organized events to occur. The exterior stairs are the physical link between the Boardwalk level of the pavilion and the lower parking lot level. However, the concrete roof above the coffee bar folds downward; it acts as a water fall to create an element that visually links the two levels. The interstitial space between this waterfall and the Tower base creates an entrance plaza for the restaurant, exhibition and office spaces. Since the roof is peeled back from the corners of the property line natural light is still able to penetrate the lower level spaces. The Pavilion composes a new space that accentuates and at the same time merges the existing urban fabric of Coney Island.

DLA Architecture: Christopher Levett, Michael Hughes, Ian Liptrot, Jorge Seperizza, Ben Stagg (London, United Kingdom)

THE MOMENT OF RELEASE

Matias Sambarino (Montevideo, Uruguay)

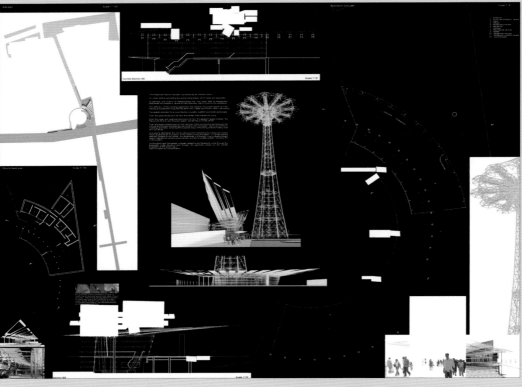

Brandon Hackett (Enid, Oklahoma)

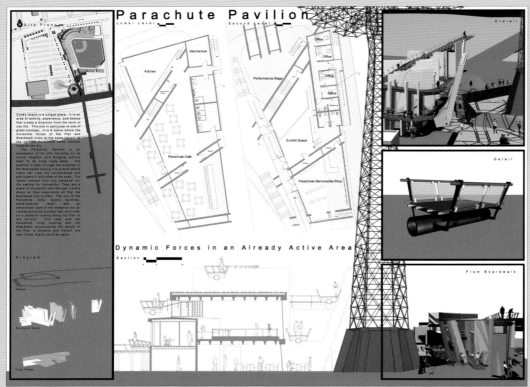

Parachute Pavilion

Dynamic Forces in an Already Active Area

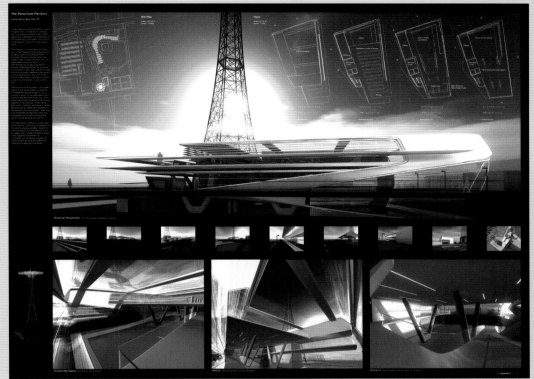

THE PARACHUTE PAVILION
CONEYISLANDNY

FTL Design Engineering Studio: Nicholas Goldsmith, Ali-Reza Razavi, Haewon Lee (New York, New York)

THE PARACHUTE PAVILION

FOOT PRINT: A rationalized geometry of site boundaries.
FORM: A portion of a torus.
STRUCTURE: A concrete shell, supported by concrete driven piles.
PROGRAM: A decked open roof surface, sheltering all programs.
SYSTEMS: High strength cast in place concrete. Cable net supported curtain wall.
CULTURE: A gently elevated plane. A point of station, of contemplation.

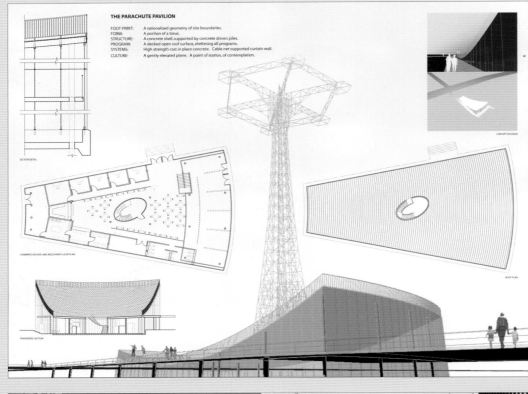

Joao Pedro Miguel, Luis Monteiro, Barbara Miguel, Pedro Viegas, Alexandre Baptista (Lisbon, Portugal)

The Firm: Alvin Chen, Edwin Liu, Felix Monasakanian, Nebi Nazar, Efren Soriano (Walnut, California)

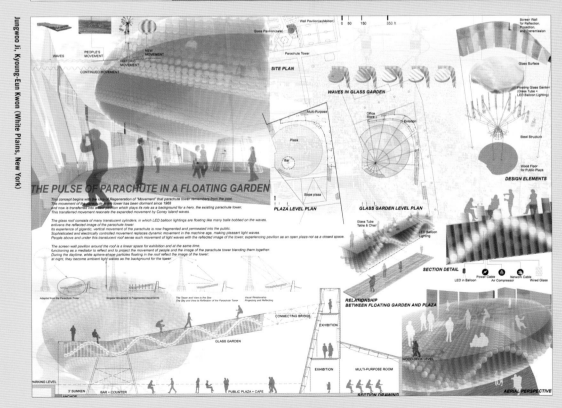

Jungwoo Ji, Kyoung-Eun Kwon (White Plains, New York)

C-CHAIZE.

THE PULSE OF PARACHUTE IN A FLOATING GARDEN

This concept begins with the idea of Regeneration of "Movement" that parachute tower remembers from the past.
The movement of the parachute in the tower has been dormant since 1968
and now is transferred into another pavilion which plays its role as a background for a hero, the existing parachute tower.
This transferred movement resonate the expanded movement by Coney Island waves.

The glass roof consists of many translucent cylinders, in which LED balloon lightings are floating like many balls bobbed on the waves.
enlivens the reflected image of the parachute tower.
Its experience of gigantic, vertical movement of the parachute is now fragmented and permeated into the public.
Sophisticated and electrically controlled movement replaces dynamic movement in the machine age, making pleasant light waves.
People above and under this translucent roof sense such movement of light waves with the reflected image of the tower, experiencing pavilion as an open plaza not as a closed space.

The screen wall pavilion around the roof is a linear space for exhibition and at the same time.
functioning as a mediator to reflect and to project the movement of people and the image of the parachute tower blending them together.
During the daytime, white sphere-shape particles floating in the roof reflect the image of the tower;
at night, they become ambient light waves as the background for the tower.

SITE PLAN

WAVES IN GLASS GARDEN

PLAZA LEVEL PLAN

GLASS GARDEN LEVEL PLAN

DESIGN ELEMENTS

SECTION DETAIL

RELATIONSHIP
BETWEEN FLOATING GARDEN AND PLAZA

SECTION DRAWING

AERIAL PERSPECTIVE

AIRSCAPE

Miso Soup Design: Daisuke Nagatomo, Minnie Jan (New York, New York)

The Parachute Pavilion:

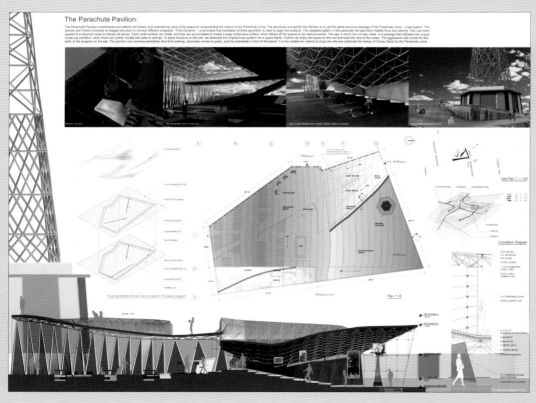

Alexandros Tsamis, Lydia Kallipoliti, Saeed Arida (Cambridge, Massachusetts)

BEACHSCAPE

From "gently rippled" surfaces to the "biggest wave on the beach," these "beachscapes" are inspired by this world-famous seaside location. These natural or synthetic landscapes, envisioned for sites below and above the boardwalk, reinvent the Coney Island beachfront for the twenty-first century.

Sofia Zuberbuhler, Jorge Yafar (New York, New York)

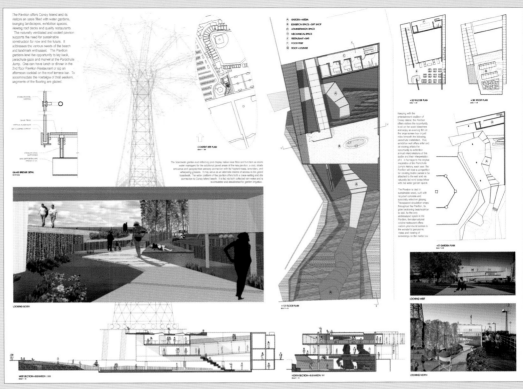

John Oldham, Xyna Cabuling, Amy Williams (Dallas, Texas)

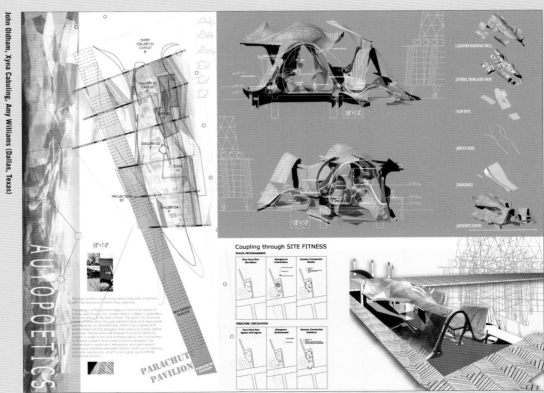

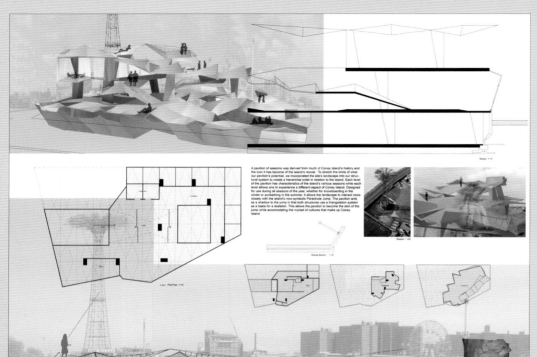

A pavilion of seasons was derived from much of Coney Island's history and the icon it has become of the island's revival. To stretch the limits of what our pavilion's potential, we incorporated the site's landscape into our structural system to create a hierarchical order in relation to the island. Each level of the pavilion has characteristics of the island's various seasons while each level allows one to experience a different aspect of Coney Island. Designed for use during all seasons of the year, whether for snowboarding in the winter or sunbathing in the summer, it allows the landscape to interact more closely with the island's now-symbolic Parachute Jump. The pavilion acts as a shadow to the jump in that both structures use a triangulation system as a basis for a skeleton. This allows the pavilion to become the skin of the jump while accomodating the myriad of cultures that make up Coney Island.

LOOPING:

entwining past, present, and future

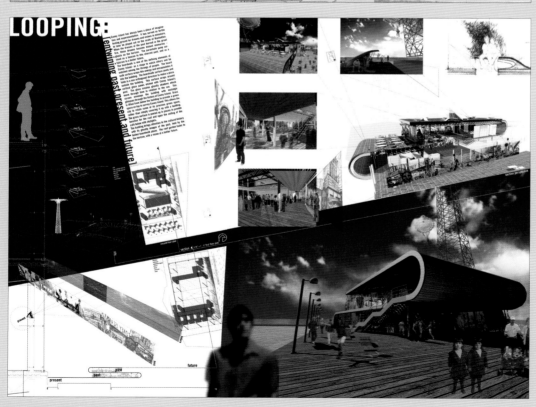

Urvaksh Aga Design: Urvaksh Aga, Fravashi Aga, Priya Malhotra, Sailee Jhadav (Bombay, India)

Two-N: Hermann Zschiegner (New York, New York)

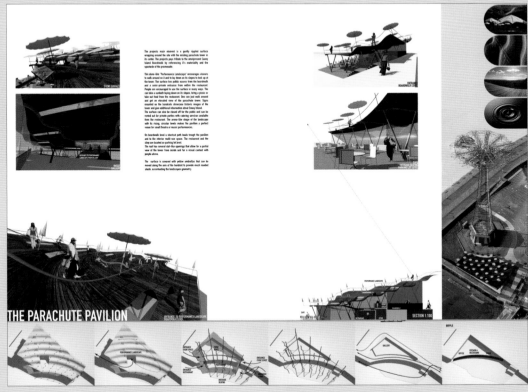

Viviana Florea (Baldwin, New York)

David Nepveux (Stillwater, Oklahoma)

PARACHUTE PAVILION: UNDER THE BOARDWALK

pavilion entry from south

restaurant entry from south

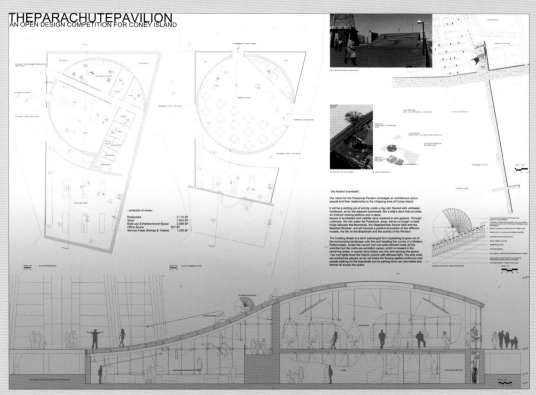

THEPARACHUTEPAVILION
AN OPEN DESIGN COMPETITION FOR CONEY ISLAND

Tiar Studio: Federico Florena, Luigi Della Morte, Francesca Vasquez, Giuseppe Meola (Napoli, Italy)

...the heated boardwalk.

Our vision for the Parachute Pavilion envisages an architecture about people and their relationship to the intriguing area of Coney Island.

It will be a melting pot of activity under a big roof, floored with untreated hardwood, as for the adjacent boardwalk, like a ship's deck that provides an inclined viewing platform and a plaza.

Issues of symbolism and visibility were resolved in one gesture. Through continuity, the site under the Parachute Jump, will be no longer a more hinge between the Boardwalk, the Steeplechase Soccer field and the Baseball Stadium, but will become a positive encounter of two different models, the life on the Boardwalk and the activity of the Pavilion.

The building shape is a semi submerged form appearing to grow out of the surrounding landscape, with the roof modeling the curves of a Modern Rollercoaster. Under the curved roof one solid element holds all the activities but the multi-use exhibition space, which is located in the remaining areas. A curved ramp draws you into and accross the space. Two roof lights flood the interior volume with diffused light. The side walls are exclusively glazed, so do not brake the flowing spatial continuum and people walking on the boardwalk and at parking level can see inside and almost all across the space.

schedule of areas:

Restaurant	3,174 SF
Store	1,905 SF
Multi-use Exhibition/event Space	2,049 SF
Office Space	527 SF
Service Areas (Ramps & Toilets)	1,236 SF

Eva Perez de Vega Steele (New York, New York)

PARACHUTE PAVILION in Coney Island

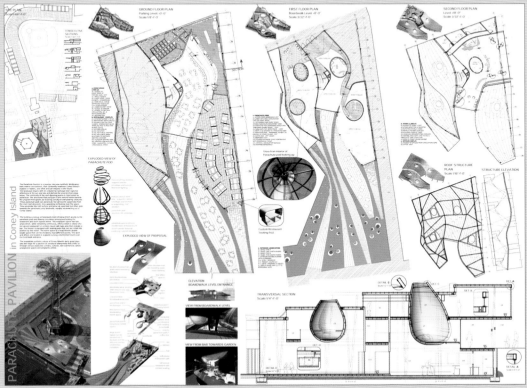

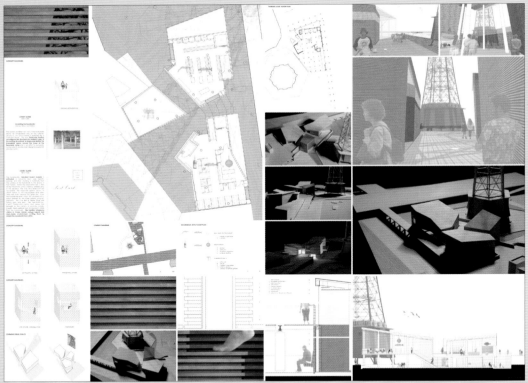

Can Tiryaki, Juan Villafañe (Cambridge, Massachusetts)

WHAT IS THE NEW PAVILION OF FUN ....

Studio 422: Devin Harvath, Steve Valev, Eric Combs, Zack Aders, Greg Wedge (Tempe, Arizona)

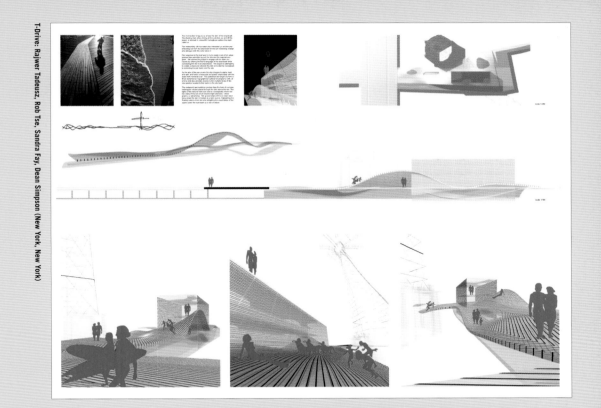

TACTILE TECH-STYLE

Fluid or frozen, fabric or wood, high-tech or low-tech, these highly stylized proposals invite you to touch. Dynamic and interactive, the sensual environments of these projects suggest new spatial experiences.

Michał Piasecki, Tomasz Waszkiewicz, Marcin Mirkowicz (Warsaw, Poland)

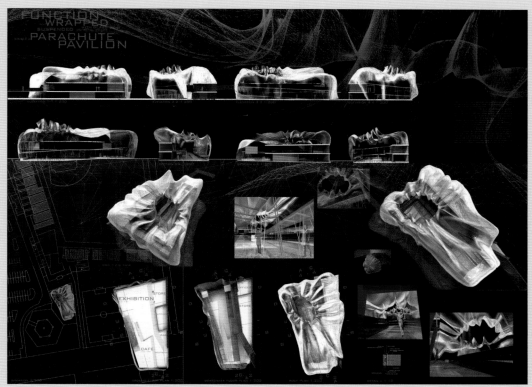

Joyce Hwang (Philadelphia, Pennsylvania)

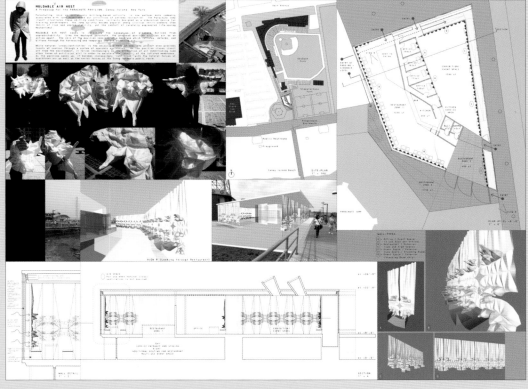

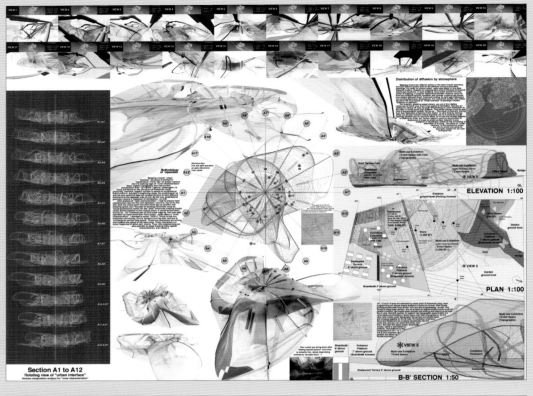

Gin Johannes Studio: Gin Johannes Konuma (Shizuoka, Japan)

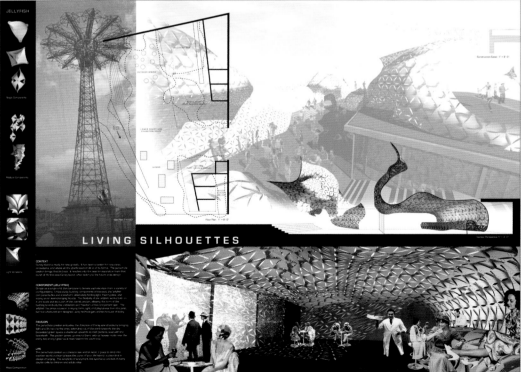

Michael Duffy, Kyle Larkin, Angela Sinclair, Dat Tran, Josh Davil, Jason Ploszaj (Tempe, Arizona)

Joseph Michael, Hannah Lippard (Raleigh, North Carolina)

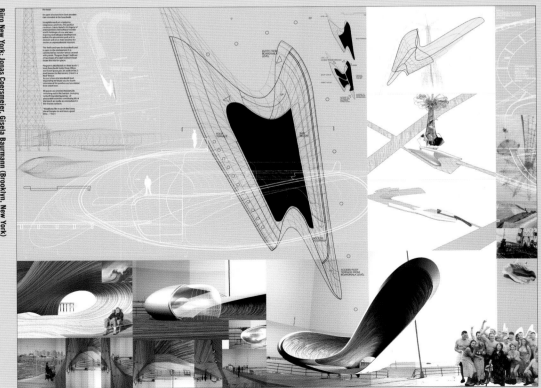

FLUID DYNAMISM

Büro New York: Jonas Coersmeier, Gisela Baurmann (Brooklyn, New York)

Michal Teller (Warsaw, Poland)

the Parachute Pavilion an open design competition for Coney Island

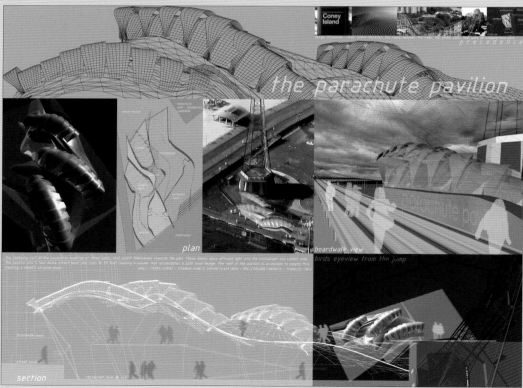

Hybridarch, Indraneel Dutta, Abhay Zachariah, Brinda Kannan (London, United Kingdom)

the parachute pavilion

Denegri Bessai Studio: Tom Bessai, Maria Denegri, Hugh Clark, Jackie To, Michael Scott, Rajan Patel (Toronto, Canada)

Motonobu Kurokawa Architecture: Motonobu Kurokawa (Oiso-machi Kanagawa-ken, Japan)

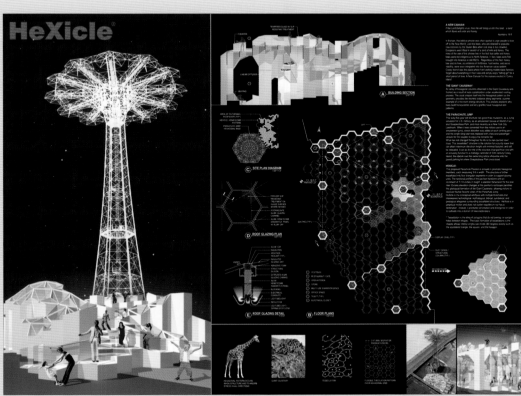

The Coney Island Pavilion:
a Flashing Glass Cage of the Sensual

The desire towards bodily pleasure has never been a taboo in Coney Island. It rather offered a stage to literally produce physical amusement and ecstasy. The imagination and the inventiveness were fully exploited to generate an instant thrill. A moment of time was, however, how long it took to fell from its dazzling legacy of "playground of the world" to the anonymous and the uncharacteristic. What we have to revive is not the physicality of the past, but the value of Coney Island that is fantastically different.

The liquid crystal roof veils the programmed post (value) under its translucent surface. The pavilion is a public spa that offers warmth to the beachgoers, the athletes and the neighborhood. The interior space gets uncovered to the surrounding by the individual actions outside. The milky white roof consists of the liquid crystal glass panels, and when a person steps on it, several panels around him/her suddenly become transparent revealing the inside. As more crowd walk on the roof, the structure loses its solidity and becomes a fleshy cage of pleasurable events.

The spatial quality of spa leans towards sensuality and openness rather than relaxation and isolation. The loud fast tempo music gets combined with the glittering effect of constantly changing light through the roof. The warm water flows along the two floors, the walls and a slide, and the private jacuzzi tubs float around them. As the roof is an extension of the boardwalk, the water inside gets stretched to the Raritan Bay and beyond.

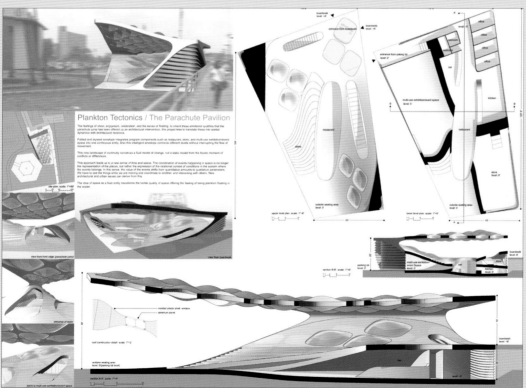

Plankton Tectonics / The Parachute Pavilion

The feelings of cheer, enjoyment, celebration, and the sense of floating, to orient these emotional qualities that the parachute jump has been offered us as architectural intervention, this project tries to translate those into spatial dynamics with architectural tectonics.

Folded and layered envelope integrates program components such as restaurant, store, and multi-use exhibition/event space into one continuous entity. Also this intelligent envelope connects different levels without interrupting the flow of movement.

This new landscape of continuity conceives a fluid model of change, not a static model from the frozen moment of conflicts or differences.

This approach leads us to a new sense of time and space. The coordination of events happening in space is no longer the representation of the places, but rather the expression of the relational context of conditions in the system where the events belongs. In this sense, the value of the events shifts from quantitative amounts to qualitative parameters. We have to see the things while we are moving one coordinate to another, and interacting with others. New architectural and urban issues can derive from this.

The idea of space as a fluid entity transforms the tactile quality of space offering the feeling of being plankton floating in the ocean.

Thaddeus Pawlowski; Julia Murphy (Brooklyn, New York)

coney island
parachute pavilion

Site: This intervention for Coney Island proposes an alternative topography for the edge of New York City.

A series of poles stand at regular intervals across the site. Ribbons of fabric (averaging about 16' by 220') hang between these poles and are anchored to the ground with cables. In homage to the ghost of the Coney Island Parachute riders these ribbons restore the experience of fabric riding on wind to this landscape. Fans are mounted on the poles to augment the lift of the wind. The ribbons gradually rise from a height 2' above the boardwalk and rise to thirty feet above the parking lot. This slope follows a canted horizon line which continues with the drop of the beach into the water. Standing on the boardwalk, this soft horizon comes into sharp contrast with the true horizon.

Below the ribbons, light and shadow play through the translucent fabric on dune grass that grows on the furrowed landscape around the Parachute Jump and the median strips in the parking lot.

Parachute Pavilion: Between the entrance of the baseball stadium and the Parachute Jump, one ribbon takes a dive toward the ground. This marks the location of the courtyard around which the parachute pavilion is organized. Entering from the parking lot, a visitor passes under a low overhang and comes out into the courtyard where the dip in the curtain frames a dizzying view of the tower. Sliding translucent fiberglass panels separate the courtyard from the surrounding spaces, a café, gallery, and office. A retail space at the top the stairs also opens up onto the stadium branch of the boardwalk.

A prayer for Coney Island...

We pray for new clothes
for the parachute jump,
cold and naked by the sea too long.

We pray that New Yorkers never
again face a flat horizon, but
continue to toss and regain
their desires in a tilted land
that drifts effortlessly upward (back up and down again).

floor plan
1/16"=1'-0"

roof plan
1:200

Etienne Feher (Paris, France)

THEPARACHUTEPAVILION:
an open design competition for Coney Island

scale in meters : Plan of the site 1/500

scale in meters : Plan 1/200

scale in meters : elevations 1/200

section 1/200

parachute built the space

1 views to the parachute jump

2 ecological ventilation

3

Nobuaki Furuya (Shinjuku-ku, Japan)

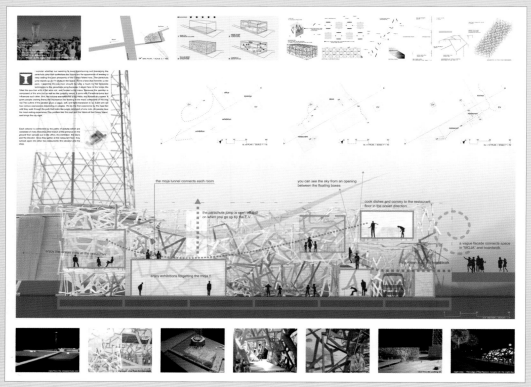

the moja tunnel connects each room

you can see the sky from an opening between the floating boxes

the parachute jump is seen off and on when you go up by the E.V.

cook dishes and convey to the restaurant floor in the ocean direction

enjoy the ocean view at the restaurant

a vague facade connects space in "MOJA" and boardwalk

enjoy exhibitions forgetting the moja !!

Luca Donner, Francesca Sorcinelli (Silea, Italy)

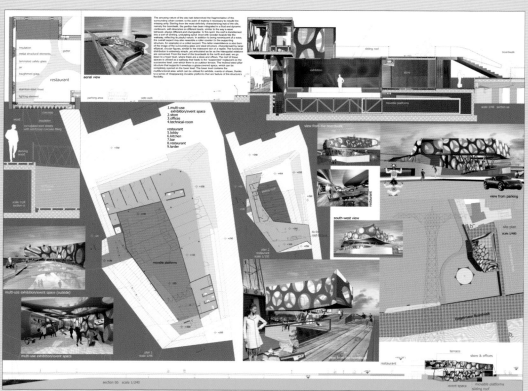

aerial view

restaurant

exhibition

sliding roof

store

boardwalk

movable platforms

view from the boardwalk

view from parking

1. multi-use exhibition/event space
2. store
3. offices
4. technical-room

restaurant
5. lobby
6. kitchen
7. bar
8. restaurant
9. larder

movable platforms

restaurant

south-west view

multi-use exhibition/event space (outside)

multi-use exhibition/event space

site plan
scale 1/480

terrace

store & offices

restaurant

event space   movable platforms
                sliding roof

section bb   scale 1/240

ZELENOPLAVO: Rikard Blazicko, Marko Jakelic, Estera Kecek, Robert Kecek, Richie Pattucci (Zagreb, Croatia)

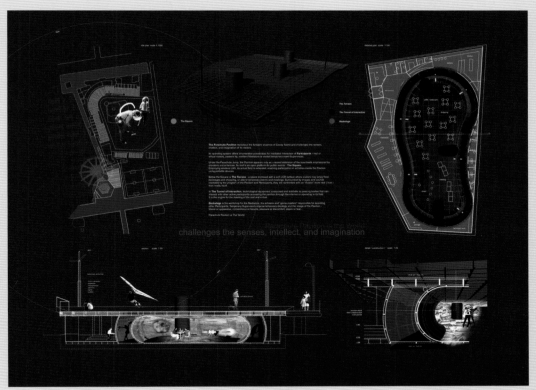

Andrew Brister, Stephen Brister (Stillwater, Oklahoma)

Parachute Pavilion: Drop into the tall grass...

The Parachute Pavilion: an Open Design Competition for Coney Island

REVERSE: Josa Ballesteros, Luis A. Alonso, Alvaro Gutierrez (Madrid, Spain)

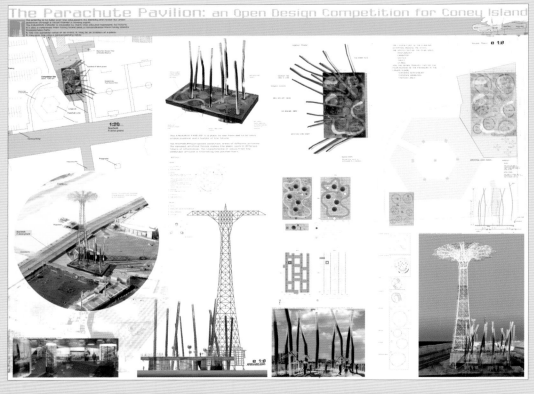

POST: Edward Richardson, April Clark, Justin Kwok, Brendan Lee (Santa Fe, New Mexico)

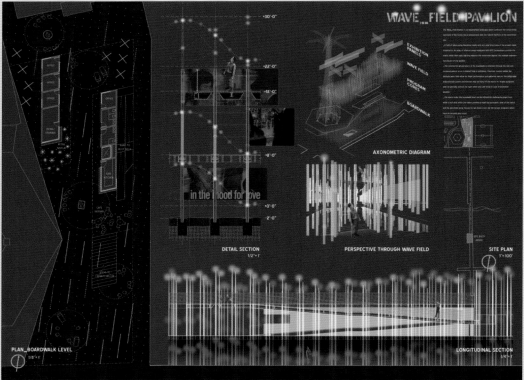

HAVE YOU SEEN THE PARACHUTE PAVILION THIS MONTH?

An Open-ended frame for Coney Island

Coney Island should be new every month

For the Parachute Pavilion, we propose a frame in the spirit of the Parachute Jump itself – it is both a collapsible structural framing system that is easy to assemble, and a framework for creativity through the installation of different uses by artists, fashion designers, lighting designers, and community members.

Parts of the frame are permanent, parts are temporary; parts are covered with skin, parts are open to air and light. Custom-designed joints and clips allow for skins of fabric, glass, metal, or almost any material to be attached to the frame. Since the frame is designed with precise, computer-milled-like slots, it is both strong and lightweight. Since it is made from standard sheets of ¾" thick plywood, it is affordable to construct and it complements the famous boardwalk.

We have tested our system for structural performance and visual effects through full-scale prototypes. Our open-ended system allows for straight or curving shapes, and our design lives like the ocean and creates outdoor and indoor spaces on two levels. We are proposing an open system and a flexible design that can accommodate changes and incorporate input from public and private ventures and residents of Coney Island. When the pavilion comes to life, with its own unique identities and its continually renewed skin, it will bring people to the area again and again.

CONEYSCOPE

These projects celebrate everything that is Coney Island. They are colorful, vibrant, and animated. They give rise to spectacle, voyeurism, and human desire and invite you to Step Right Up!

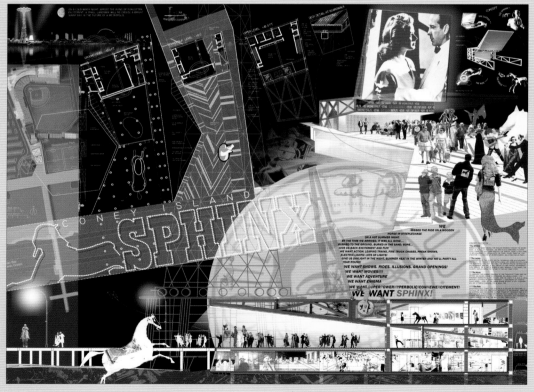

MERA Design: Aleksandr Mergold, Yuriy Mergold, Boris Ravvin (Brooklyn, New York)

Tiburon: Daniel Holguin, Natalia Porter, Eduardo Ramos (New York, New York)

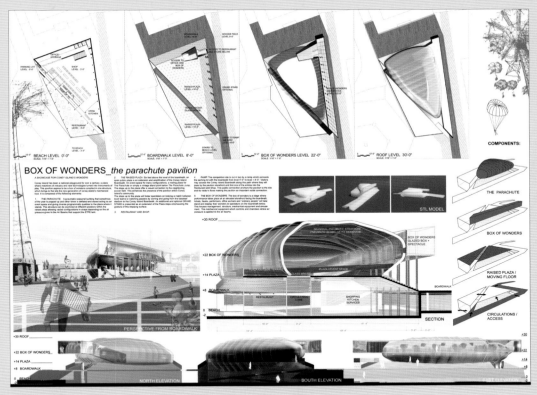

BOX OF WONDERS_*the parachute pavilion*

Amanda Glidewell (Lubbock, Texas)

You know you want to look

"Tilyou had discovered that customers would pay for the privilege of entertaining other customers."

Lyle Estanislao, Erica D'Almeida (Newark, New Jersey)

REDEFINING CONEY ISLAND
REINTERPRETING AMUSEMENT
REINSERTING SPECTACLE

Escapism has been the driving force for the development of Coney Island, exploiting an optimal natural condition for the creation of an artificial environment that satisfies specific social demands. Coney Island became a construct of isolated enclosures with an amusement typology defined by the human desire to participate in experiences that are void of moral consequence. This "pavilion" simply provides these opportunities, and therefore becomes an arena for deviant behavior, achieving the satisfaction of social demand as a by-product of exploiting human nature. Taking a cue from historic Coney Island, this interior condition provides an isolated environment away from external influence, which results in the loss of reservation for the gain of primal desire. There is a schism between exterior and interior, a play on both the disconnect between social facade and inner desire, as well as the differing moral connotations of day and night. The exterior is active during the day, acting as a glorified boardwalk with views towards the ocean. The interior comes alive at night, providing dark corners for dark deeds.

THE VOYEUR

THE EXHIBITIONIST

THE FETISHIST

THE FLIRT

THE SWINGER

SOCIAL FACADE
PROTECTION
PUBLIC
DAY

INNER DESIRE
EXPOSURE
INTIMATE
NIGHT

SIGHT SOUND
+
SMELL TASTE
+
TOUCH

THE "PAVILION"_ DAYTIME

THE "PAVILION"_ NIGHTTIME

SECTIONAL DIAGRAM

SECTION PERSPECTIVE

CONEY ISLAND AND THE PAVILION ARE ONLY THE ARENA...THE PEOPLE ARE THE SPECTACLE AND AMUSEMENT

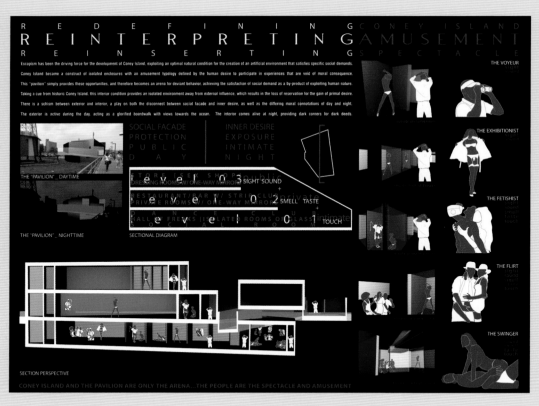

Mads Mandrup Hansen, Morten Vedelsbol (Frederiksberg, Denmark)

THE PARACHUTE PAVILION

The basic form of the pavilion takes its inspiration from its impressive structural counterpoint on the site.

The powerful and potent vertical steel grid structure of the parachute jump inspired us to pursue similar simplicity and clarity in our building, which both could communicate with the towering presence of its impressive neighbor and at the same time encapsulate the essence of its historical and contemporary context—a tribute to the family of amusement.

Super Superficial: Sang Hoon Lee, Alastair Townsend (London, United Kingdom)

Coney Island Wedding Plaza

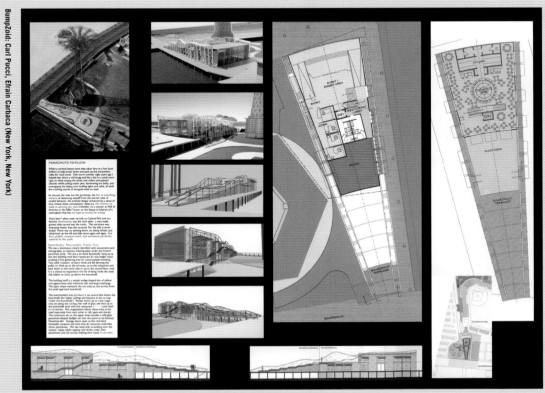

BumpZoid: Carl Pucci, Efrain Carbaca (New York, New York)

PARACHUTE PAVILION

Identifiable, Mountable, Public, Fun

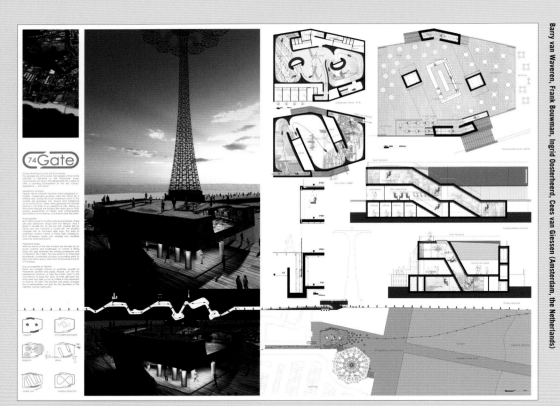

Barry van Waveren, Frank Bouwman, Ingrid Oosterheerd, Cees van Giessen (Amsterdam, the Netherlands)

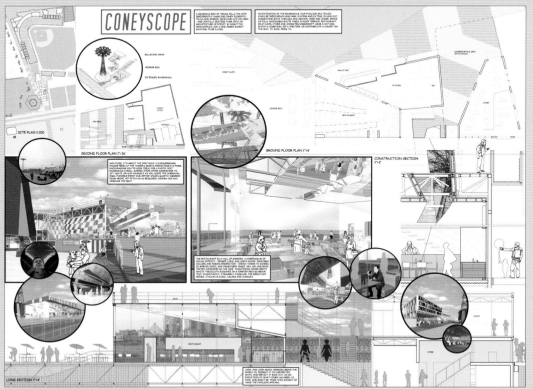

AOC: Tom Coward, Daisy Froud, Vincent Lacovara, Geoff Shearcroft (London, United Kingdom)

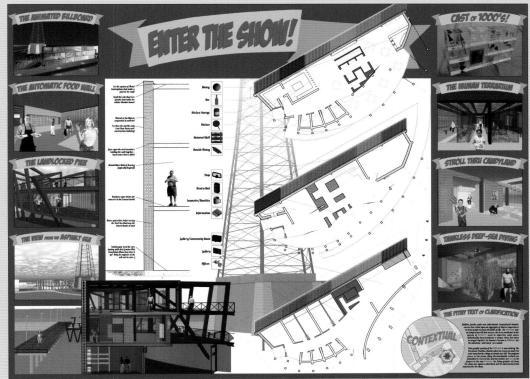

Tilder Studio: Miller + Strogney: Mark Miller, Stephanie Strogney, Lisa Tilder (Instructor) (Columbus, Ohio)

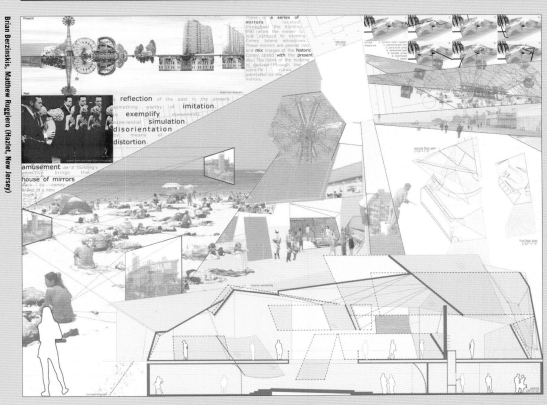

Brian Berzinskis, Matthew Ruggiero (Hazlet, New Jersey)

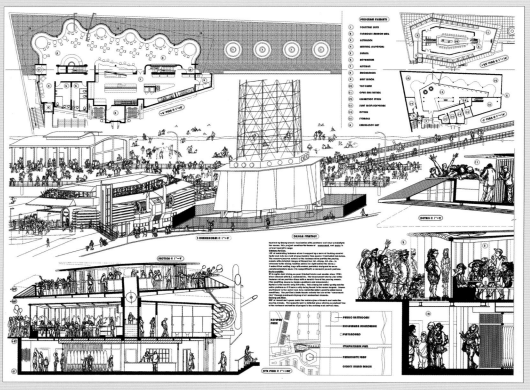

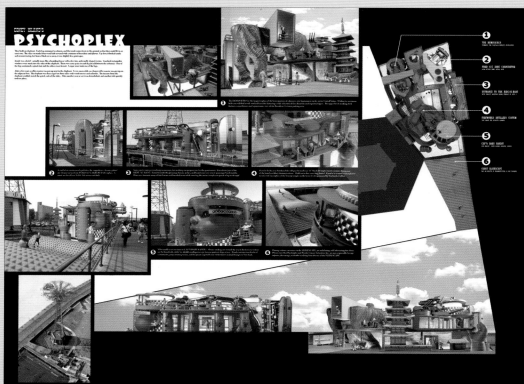

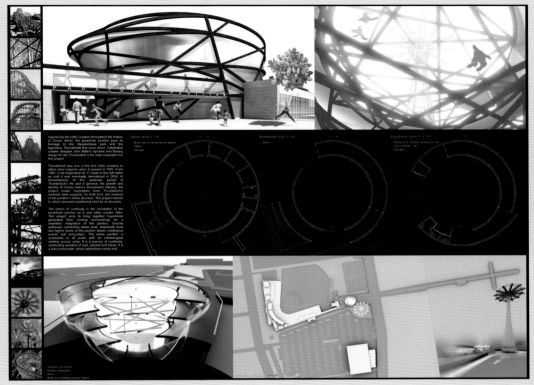

Inspired by the roller coasters throughout the history of Coney Island, the parachute pavilion pays its homage to the Steeplechase park and the legendary Thunderbolt that once stood. Celebrated coaster designer John Miller's dynamic and flowing design for the Thunderbolt is the main inspiration for this project.

Thunderbolt was one of the first roller coasters to utilize steel supports when it opened in 1925. From 1983, it sat inoperative for 17 years in the sun-ridden air until it was eventually demolished in 2000. In remembrance of this particular period of Thunderbolt's life and in general, the growth and decline of Coney Island's amusement industry, the project draws inspirations from Thunderbolt's oxidized steel supports, for both form and material of the pavilion's entire structure. The project intends to utilize uncoated weathering steel for its structure.

The notion of continuity is the foundation of the parachute pavilion as it any roller coaster rides. The project aims to bring together trajectories generated from existing surroundings for a seamless integration of the pavilion. Diverse pathways connecting street level, boardwalk level and higher levels of the pavilion spawn continuous events and encounters. The entire pavilion is accessible to all public with an uninterrupted swirling access ramp. It is a journey of continuity, connecting wonders of past, present and future. It is a wild promenade, where adventures never end.

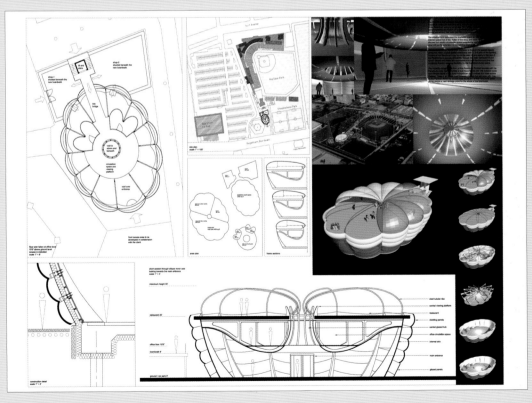

PARACHUTE PAVILION, CONEY ISLAND

Rommelaere&Lacronique: Antoine Lacronique, Philippe Rommelaere (Paris, France)

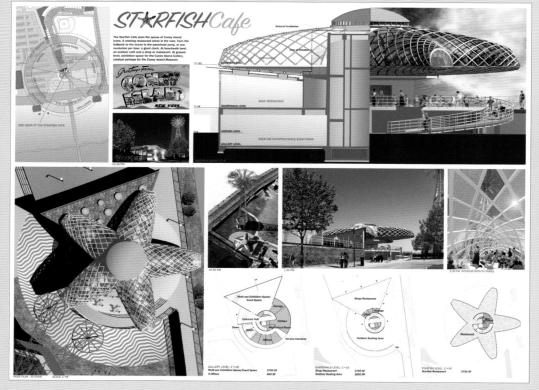

Michael Sorkin Studio: Michael Sorkin, Britta Degn, Makoto Okazaki (New York, New York)

STARFISH Cafe

Nicolas D'Angelo (Cambridge, Massachusetts)

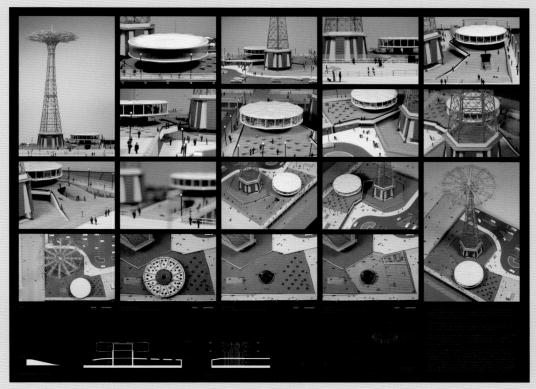

Next Phase Studios, Inc.: Rick Ames; Anabela Niedda; Elizabeth Stifel; Martin Werminghausen; Lisa Hiserodt; Rick Ames (Jamaica Plain, Massachusetts)

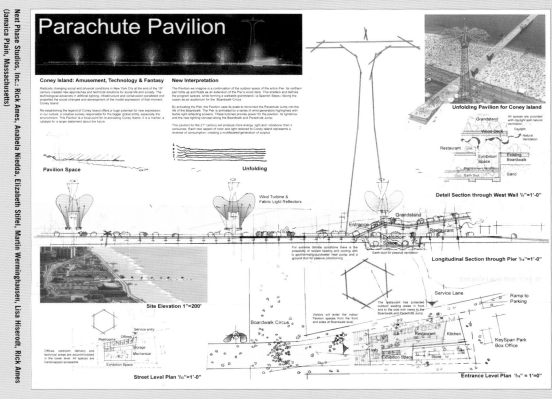

EXTENDING THE BOARDWALK

Approximately eighty feet wide and two miles long, the Riegelman Boardwalk stretches along the beach. These proposals break this linear pattern and explore the materiality and physicality of the boardwalk by ramping, folding, elevating, and extending its form to and from the given site.

Seijo Arquitectos y Asociados S.C.P.: Juan Seijo, Arturo Carrillo, Eduardo Puerto, Victor Cruz, Josefina Peon (Merida, Mexico)

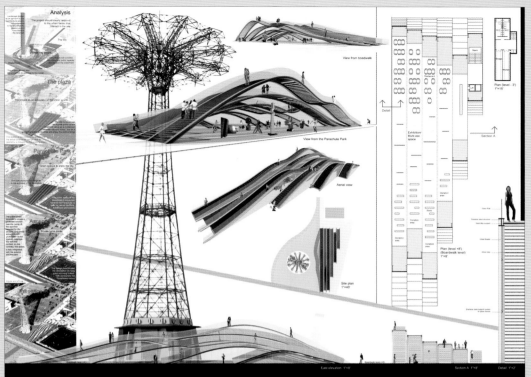

Scarano and Associates Architects: Robert Scarano Jr., Alexander Zhitnik, Orlando Garcia, Samira Yaghmai, Daniel Mecuci (Brooklyn, New York)

LOOP-D-LOOP

Parachute Pavilion

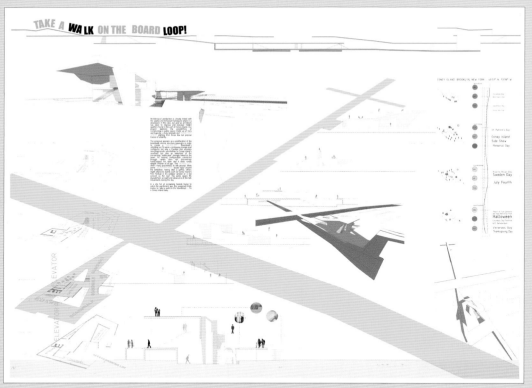

KTDN: Isabel Benito, Victor Orive, Santiago Becerra (Madrid, Spain)

TAKE A **WA**LK ON THE BOARD **LOOP!**

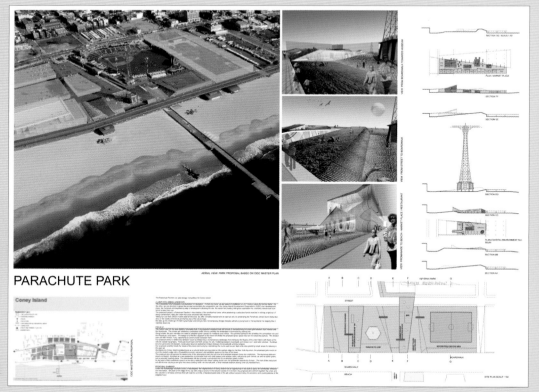

Todo Design and Werner: Silva Ajemian, Jorge Prado, Stefanie Werner (New York, New York)

PARACHUTE PARK

Coney Island

AERIAL VIEW: PARK PROPOSAL BASED ON ODC MASTER PLAN

Trevor Thimm, Pauline Alam (Cambridge, Massachusetts)

Hackenbroich Architects: Wilfried Hackenbroich, Rainer Muehr (Berlin, Germany)

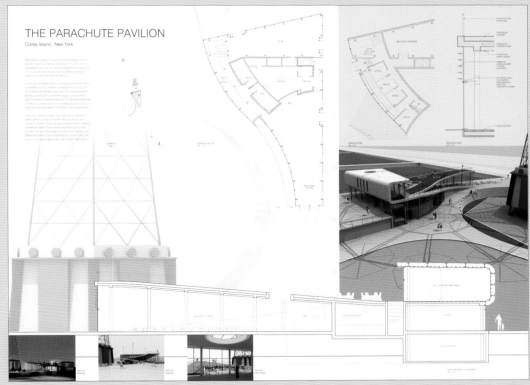

THE PARACHUTE PAVILION

Coney Island New York

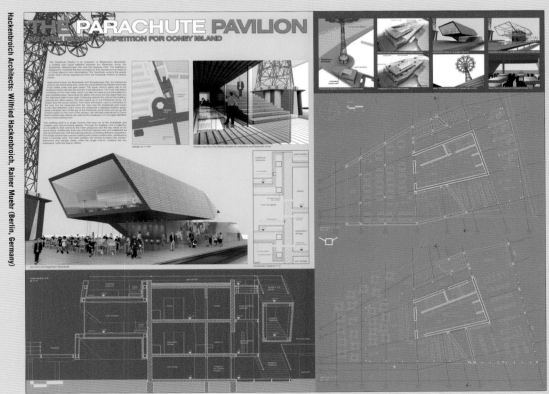

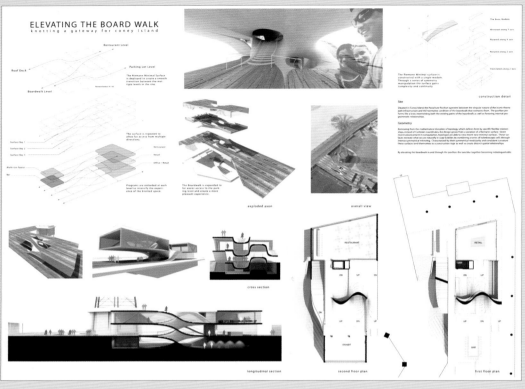

ELEVATING THE BOARD WALK
knotting a gateway for coney island

exploded axon

overall view

construction detail

cross section

longitudinal section

second floor plan

first floor plan

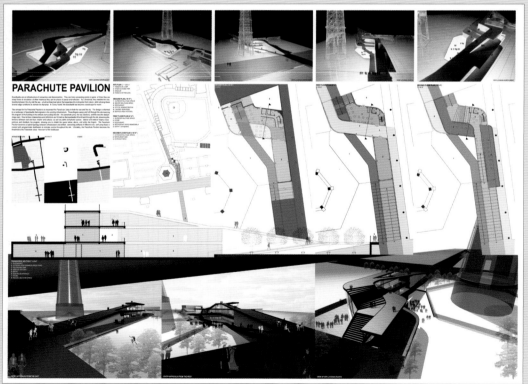

PARACHUTE PAVILION

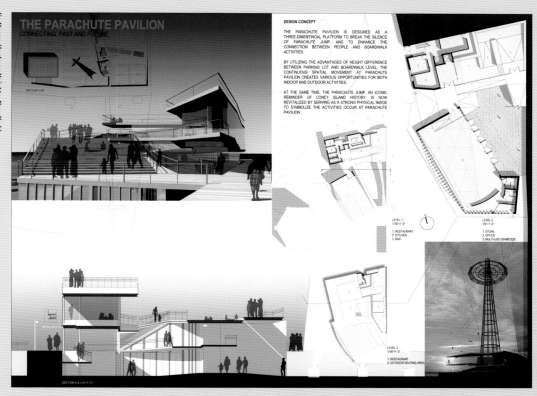

THE PARACHUTE PAVILION
CONNECTING PAST AND FUTURE

DESIGN CONCEPT

THE PARACHUTE PAVILION IS DESIGNED AS A THREE-DIMENTIONAL PLATFORM TO BREAK THE SILENCE OF PARACHUTE JUMP, AND TO ENHANCE THE CONNECTION BETWEEN PEOPLE AND BOARDWALK ACTIVITIES.

BY UTILIZING THE ADVANTAGES OF HEIGHT DIFFERENCE BETWEEN PARKING LOT AND BOARDWALK LEVEL, THE CONTINUOUS SPATIAL MOVEMENT AT PARACHUTE PAVILION CREATES VARIOUS OPPORTUNITIES FOR BOTH INDOOR AND OUTDOOR ACTIVITIES.

AT THE SAME TIME, THE PARACHUTE JUMP, AN ICONIC REMINDER OF CONEY ISLAND HISTORY, IS NOW REVITALIZED BY SERVING AS A STRONG PHYSICAL IMAGE TO SYMBOLIZE THE ACTIVITIES OCCUR AT PARACHUTE PAVILION.

Jie Huang (Jackson Heights, New York)

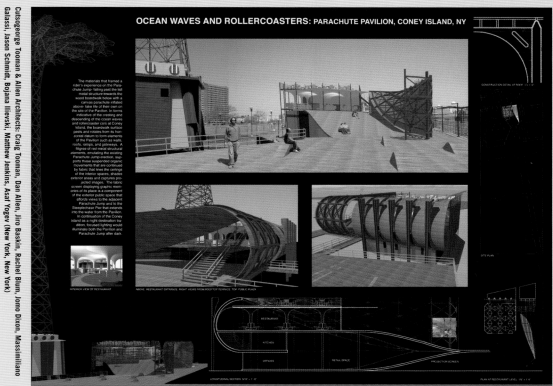

OCEAN WAVES AND ROLLERCOASTERS: PARACHUTE PAVILION, CONEY ISLAND, NY

The materials that framed a rider's experience on the Parachute Jump- falling past the tall metal structure towards the wood boardwalk below with a canvas parachute inflated above- take life of their own on the site of the Pavilion. In forms indicative of the cresting and descending of the ocean waves and rollercoaster cars at Coney Island, the boardwalk surface peels and rotates from its horizontal datum to form elements of the Pavilion such as walls, roofs, ramps, and gateways. A filigree of red metal structural elements, emulating the existing Parachute Jump erection, supports these suspended organic movements that are continued by fabric that lines the ceilings of the interior spaces, shades exterior areas and captures projected images. The fabric screen displaying graphic memories of its place is a component of the exterior public space that affords views to the adjacent Parachute Jump and to the Steeplechase Pier that extends into the water from the Pavilion. In continuation of the Coney Island as a night destination tradition, focused lighting would illuminate both the Pavilion and Parachute Jump after dark.

Cutsogeorge Tooman & Allen Architects; Craig Tooman, Dan Allen, Jiro Baskin, Rachel Blum, Jomo Dixon, Massimiliano Galassi, Jason Schmidt, Bojana Ilievski, Matthew Jenkins, Asaf Yogev (New York, New York)

Andrew Maynard Architect: Andrew Maynard, Matt McClurg, CI Koay (Fitzroy North, Australia)

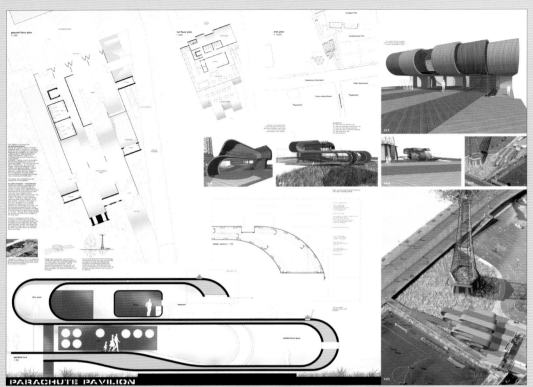

Elizabeth Bouchard, Catherine St-Marseille, Hubert Pelletier, Eric Boucher (Montreal, Canada)

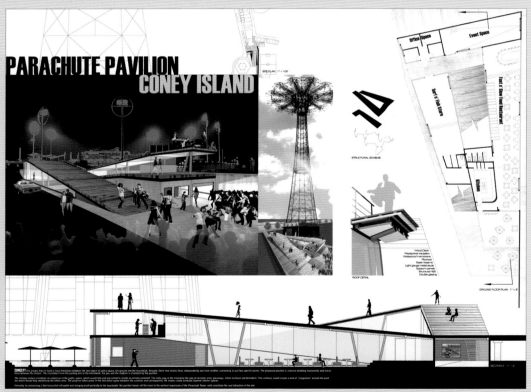

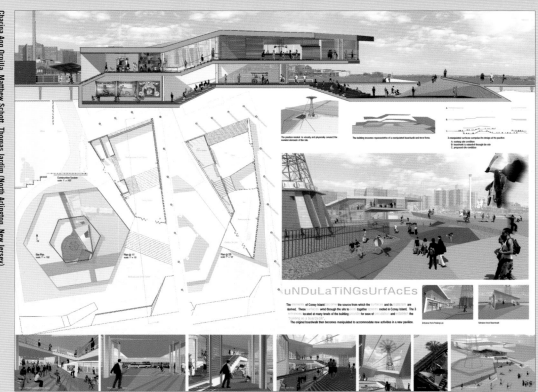

Deljana Iossifova, Rolf Demmler (Shanghai, China)

views towards surf avenue

entrance to keyspan park

+2.45 m

delivery
0.00 m

(underneath)
kitchen
-0.50 m

(underneath)
toilets
0.00 m

shop
-0.50 m

bar/exhibition
lounge
-0.50 m

office
spaces
+0.50 m

restaurant/
lounge smoking
(underneath
exhibition)
+1.45 m

pavilion square

detailed section, 1:25

floor plan, 1:100

NARRIOCH – THE GHOST OF THE MISSING SHADOW

A LONG TIME AGO, THE AREA OF CONEY ISLAND WAS REFERRED TO BY THE LOCAL TRIBES AS "NARRIOCH, THE PLACE WITHOUT SHADOWS" BECAUSE AT SUCH A PLACE WITHOUT SHADOWS TIME NATURALLY BECOMES IRRELEVANT. IT IS A SURREAL AND EVOCATIVE PLACE. NARRIOCH IS MAGIC. EVER SINCE, THIS PLACE HAS BEEN ABOUT DISSOLVING IN A PARALLEL, ALTERNATIVE, COUNTER – WORLD.

OUR DESIGN AIMS TO CAPTURE THE GHOST OF THE MISSING SHADOW IN ONE SINGLE STRUCTURE: THE PARACHUTE PAVILION. MUCH MORE THAN JUST ANOTHER EVENT TO BE ADDED TO THE SCATTERED PAST AND NEW ATTRACTIONS, IT IS, FIRST OF ALL, A PUBLIC SQUARE – AT THE MOST PROMINENT POINT OF THE FAMED BOARDWALK. STRETCHING FROM THE WOODEN DECK OF THE SEASIDE WALKWAY, IT FORMS AN UNPRETENTIOUS EVENT TOPOGRAPHY – EQUALLY EVOCATIVE TO THE SURFER, THE TOURIST AND THE FUTURE VISITOR, WHATEVER HIS INTENTION MAY BE. THE PAVILION'S ORIENTATION, DIRECTIONS AND VIEWS ARE DERIVED FROM ITS STUNNING LOCATION RIGHT UNDERNEATH THE PARACHUTE TOWER, OVERLOOKING THE STEEPLECHASE PIER AND THE SEA.

IN THE RUPTURES AND FOLDS OF THIS TOPOGRAPHY, LIGHT ITSELF BECOMES THE DESIGN EVENT:

THE PAVILION IS AS SUCH THE CULMINATION OF THE PLACE WITHOUT SHADOWS' PUBLIC SPACE.
THE PAVILION CAPTURES THE SPIRIT OF THE PLACE, IT IS NOT A VENUE OR EVENT.
THE PAVILION CELEBRATES ITSELF, IT ANCHORS AND EXPRESSES THE SENSUAL MAGIC OF THE PLACE.
THE PAVILION AIMS TO BECOME THE PLACE WITHOUT SHADOWS' LIVING SOUL, ITS MEMORY AND HEARTBEAT.

PARACHUTE JUMP

STEEPLECHASE PIER

+ 7.00m

+ 3.45m

Restaurant

Glas Railing

translucent panels

+ 2.40m

Pavilion Square

longitudinal section through bar and
exhibition lounge, 1:50

Bar / Exhibition Lounge

Exhibition Space   - 0,50m

Corridor

WC

+/- 0.000m

Charina Ann Orpilla, Matthew Schott, Thomas Jardim (North Arlington, New Jersey)

The pavilion works to visually and physically connect the
isolated elements of the site.

The building becomes representative of a manipulated boardwalk and more forms.

uNDuLaTiNGsUrfAcEs

The original boardwalk then becomes manipulated to accommodate new activities in a new pavilion.

Area Architecture: Glenn Wilcox, Anca Trandafirescu (Eugene, Oregon)

UNDER THE BOARDWALK
coney island parachute pavilion
2005 new york prize design competion

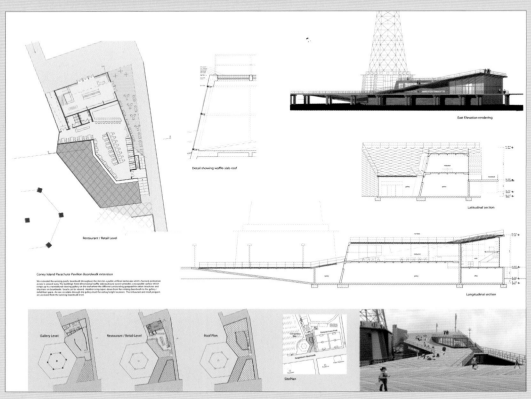

Cleanroom, Inc.: David Winston, Lisa Pauli, Robert Morris (New York, New York)

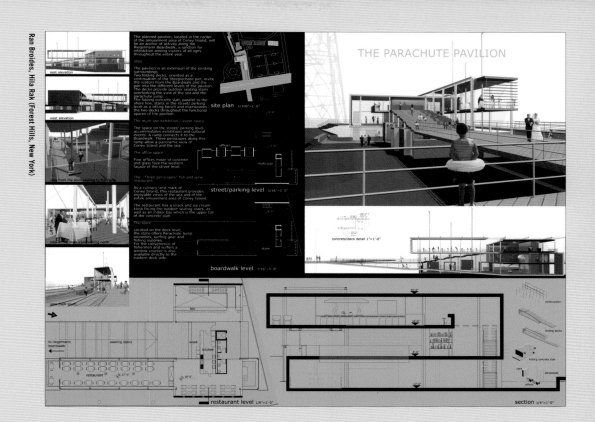

THE PARACHUTE PAVILION

The planned pavilion, located in the center of the amusement area of Coney Island, will be an anchor of activity along the Riegelmann boardwalk, a junction for interaction among visitors of all ages throughout the entire year.

Idea

The pavilion is an extension of the existing surroundings.
Two folding decks, oriented as a continuation of the Steeplechase pier, invite the visitors from the Boardwalk and the pier into the different levels of the pavilion.
The decks provide outdoor seating stairs overlooking the view of the sea and the parachute jump.
The folding concrete slab, parallel to the shore line, starts in the street/ parking level as a sitting bench and interweaves the two decks throughout the functional spaces of the pavilion.

The multi-use exhibition / event space

The space on the street/ parking level accommodates exhibitions and cultural events. A ramp connects it to the Boardwalk. Three periscopes along this ramp allow a panoramic view of Coney Island and the sea.

The office space

Four offices made of concrete and glass face the western facade of the street level.

The "Three periscopes" fish and wine restaurant

As a culinary land mark of Coney Island, this restaurant provides enjoyable views of the sea and of the entire amusement area of Coney Island.

The restaurant has a snack and ice cream kiosk facing the outdoor seating stairs, as well as an indoor bar which is the upper tail of the concrete slab.

The store

Located on the deck level, the store offers Parachute Jump souvenirs, surfing gear and fishing supplies.
For the convenience of fishermen and surfers a window counter is also available directly to the eastern deck side.

east elevation

west elevation

site plan 1/100"=1'-0"

street/parking level 1/16"=1'-0"

boardwalk level 1/16"=1'-0"

concrete/deck detail 1"=1'-0"

restaurant level 1/8"=1'-0"

section 1/4"=1'-0"

BEYOND THE BRIEF

These projects embrace fantasy, provocation, sensationalism, or simply go "out of bounds" beyond the competition's programmatic and physical requirements. By changing, breaking, or simply ignoring the rules, these proposals make bold statements.

Superkontext: Karsten Buchholz, Daniela Bergmann (Rotterdam, the Netherlands)

Elevation West Front Back

EVIL CUSTOMS

Transformation Floorplan Detail 1:2

CONEY ISLAND RIDE

Coney Island, a world of amazement in which multiple attractions, bright colours and hotdogs compete for attention. Here, the Parachute Jump is king.

The Parachute Bar drives into this context of biking and entertainment and parks in front of the Parachute Jump. One attention getter against another. The steel tower's vertical motion is counterpointed by the horizontal movement of our customized mining truck —a blend of Airstream Motorhome, monster truck and pimped-up glam-mobile. The multi-season Parachute Bar, cruises gently along the pier, attracting cries of delight and, of course, long queues of daytrippers eager to climb aboard. But there is more to the Parachute bar than simply being the place to 'hang out'. Its versatility reflects the wide range of Coney Island attractions and therefore it has no problem serving as a café or bar; acting as head car for the Mermaid Parade or being hired out for weddings and private parties. It can just as well take passengers down to the beach for fishing, surfing as it can stage an open-air concert.

Jenny Welton (Lubbock, Texas)

Scheme to gather people for fire testing 6 p.m.

Photomontage of building in existing high rises 12 p.m.

Redline plan in +5 years

Imagine a structure light as popcorn but larger than the drop
As seen from aerial photograph top
Buffering in the sky structurally equip to stay lit
Historical traces beneath assimilate a burning kit, burn baby burn
And to resolve this exigent emergency, kick it to the hot spot
hot spot
We reflect in the flames 'cause that's a fire what we all gotta go
'Cause that's a fire what we all gotta go
And gather close around great bonfires as a humanity
Of every high tide comes a mass assembly of partisans
on bended knee
From the aggregate fires come distinctive traces
by design of smoke and flame
On the edifice and groundwork a new day will ignite
Earth, Wind and Fire wanna use water
Gonna tell a story morning glory all about the serpentine fire
Douse the flames in the summer to keep feelin' higher
Kick it to the hot spot larger than the drop

Eastside
Boardwalk
Overhang

Perspective in
First Year

FIRE!

Plan and change in five years 1"=4'

Axonometric
after
Second Year

N

boardwalk Exhibition Firestarter 1 Gift Shop Office Restaurant Exhibition Exhibition Gift Shop Office Restaurant Exhibition

Claudia Lucchini, Luca Parmeggiani, Joan Ramon Pascuets i Iglesias, Monica Mosset i Gou (London, United Kingdom)

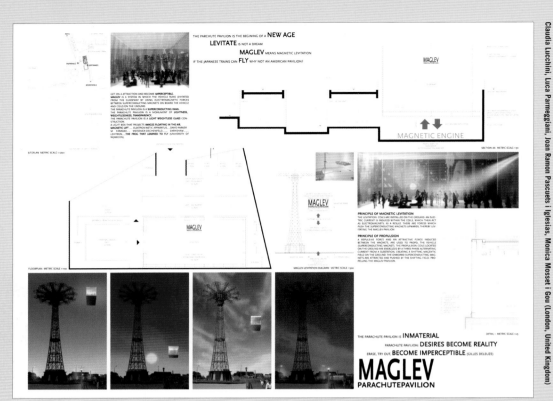

THE PARCHUTE PAVILION IS THE BEGINING OF A **NEW AGE**

LEVITATE IS NOT A DREAM

MAGLEV MEANS MAGNETIC LEVITATION

IF THE JAPANESE TRAINS CAN **FLY** WHY NOT AN AMERICAN PAVILION?

GET ON A ATTRACTION AND BECOME **IMPERCEPTIBLE.**
MAGLEV IS A SYSTEM IN WHICH THE VEHICLE RUNS LEVITATED FROM THE GUIDEWAY BY USING ELECTROMAGNETIC FORCES BETWEEN SUPERCONDUCTING MAGNETS ON BOARD THE VEHICLE AND COILS ON THE GROUND.
THE PARACHUTE PAVILION IS A **SUPERCONDUCTING MAIN.**
THE PARACHUTE PAVILION IS A MONUMENT OF **LIGHTNESS, WEIGHTLESSNESS, TRANSPARENCY.**
THE PARACHUTE PAVILION IS A **LIGHT WEIGHTLESS GLASS** CONSTRUCTION.
A LIGHT BOX THAT PROJECTS **IMAGES FLOATING IN THE AIR.**
MAGNETIC LIFT ... ELECTROKINETIC APPARATUS ... DAVID PARKER M. FARADAY ... WISSENER-OSCHENFELD ... EARNSHAW ... LEVITRON ... **THE FROG THAT LEARNED TO FLY** (UNIVERSITY OF NIJMEGEN).

MAGNETIC ENGINE

SECTION AA METRIC SCALE 1:50

SITEPLAN METRIC SCALE 1:1000

FLOORPLAN METRIC SCALE 1:100

MAGLEV LEVITATION DIAGRAM METRIC SCALE 1:1000

PRINCIPLE OF MAGNETIC LEVITATION
THE LEVITATION COILS ARE INSTALLED ON THE GROUND. AN ELECTRIC CURRENT IS INDUCED WITHIN THE COILS, WHICH THEN ACT AS ELECTROMAGNETS. AS A RESULT, THERE ARE FORCES WHICH PUSH THE SUPERCONDUCTING MAGNETS UPWARDS, THEREBY LEVITATING THE MAGLEV PAVILION.

PRINCIPLE OF PROPULSION
A REPULSIVE FORCE AND AN ATTRACTIVE FORCE INDUCED BETWEEN THE MAGNETS ARE USED TO PROPEL THE VEHICLE (SUPERCONDUCTING MAGNET). THE PROPULSION COILS LOCATED ON THE GROUND ARE ENERGIZED BY A THREE-PHASE ALTERNATING CURRENT FROM A SUBSTATION, CREATING A SHIFTING MAGNETIC FIELD ON THE GROUND. THE ONBOARD SUPERCONDUCTING MAGNETS ARE ATTRACTED AND PUSHED BY THE SHIFTING FIELD, PROPELLING THE MAGLEV PAVILION.

DETAIL 1 METRIC SCALE 1:25

THE PARACHUTE PAVILION IS **INMATERIAL**

PARACHUTE PAVILION: **DESIRES BECOME REALITY**

ERASE, TRY OUT, **BECOME IMPERCEPTIBLE** (GILLES DELEUZE)

MAGLEV
PARACHUTEPAVILION

Regin Schwaen (Blacksburg, Virginia)

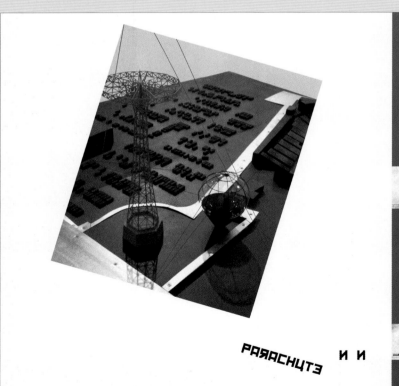

PARACHUTE

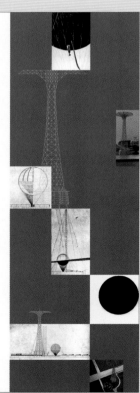

THE PARACHUTE PAVILION

The history of Coney Island has long been characterized by contrast.

The site of the first roller coaster in 1884 and the locus of America's first "holiday weekend" was also a haven for people born with disfiguring birthmarks and skin diseases like Fifi the Sheep-headed Girl, Alzoria the Turtle Girl and Sam Smith the Human Ostrich. Nathan's hot dogs and the Shoot-the-Chutes attracted middle class America but also drew visitors like Rita Hayworth and the King of England. The amusement area was struck by a series of tragic fires beginning in 1907 that forced the reimagining of the site, but the area continues to be marked by its ability to support seemingly irreconcilable images of New York City, and also of America.

Although only the Cyclone, the Wonder Wheel, and Astroland remain, there are still two different Coney Islands. The 250-foot Parachute Jump captured the spirit and freedom of the site. Two-seated passengers were pulled into the air and then released for a 20-foot freefall until the parachute filled with air and floated back down to earth. The proposal aims to capture the thrill and liberation implied by being suspended vertically in the air through the program of a balloon launch.

This program allows an aerial consideration of the contrasting images of the site while capturing the sense of vertigo that drew visitors to Coney Island's roller coasters and amusements. The adjacent service pavilion and park evoke the celebrated cacophony of Coney Island through the quotation of signage along the boardwalk and indigenous site materials. The field of circles, planted with various materials including asphalt, infield grass, sand, fragmities, composite wood and concrete, captures the Coney Island of the present. In the absence of a hot air balloon, the launch itself returns to this field of circles, becoming part of a landscape from which to appreciate and understand the dynamic ecology of the site.

THE PARACHUTE PAVILION:
an *annual* design competition for Coney Island

Throughout Coney Island's history, its various dynamic attractions have brought it to international recognition. This proposal is an attempt to recapture that dynamicism and "fun" by making this site an architectural focal point, which supports community functions while fostering architectural innovation. By sponsoring an annual competition at this site for a temporary structure, Coney Island will once again be a prevailing location for ever changing attractions. The participants in this competition will be asked to produce an avant-garde architecture with a limited lifespan: 365 days [or 366 if the competition falls on a leap year]. This competition will not only attract talented young designers, but an international audience, and maybe some older designers as well. Winners will be selected by an international jury comprised of community members, architects, landscape designers, urban designers, urban planners, and children. Due to the lack of architecture suggested through this proposal, we encourage another temporary proposal to be selected until the second annual competition can be held.

Jeannie Kim (New York, New York)

Kyle May (Wadsworth, Ohio)

Dustin Chesnutt (Lubbock, Texas)

(Insert Clever Title Here)

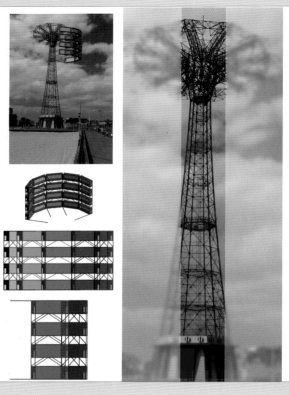

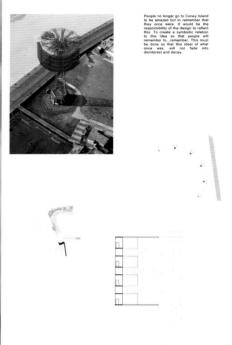

People no longer go to Coney Island to be amazed but to remember that they once were. It would be the responsibility of the design to reflect this. To create a symbiotic relation to this idea so that people will remember to...remember. This must be done so that this ideal of what once was, will not fade into disinterest and decay.

Vydavy Sindikat, Misha Sklar, Zhenya Plechkina (Brooklyn, New York)

E N T E R T A I N M E N T   U N K N □ W N

What makes all these people come to this place everyday? What makes them stay in big crowded line in strange monotonous space?
Space without any features - only long boardwalk squeezed between cruel uninterrupted concrete walls?
The only thing you see is the back of the head of the person in front of you, and far from you - the tower. You came here like people you know came here yesterday. Did you see them afterwards?
   -Excuse me, do you know, how long do we wait?
You have million other questions, but will you get answers? Does person in front of you know the answer?
   -Where is it?
- It's right there. Under the tower. Do you see it?
- Oh, I see.
You could not see it, like the man you asked could not see. But you started to play the game. You wanted this game. TV, radio, Internet, papers, flyers under your door, add on the back of your metrocard - they all wanted you here.
Do you, do you ... ping-pong ball in your head. It is not late yet, you can still turn back -
THERE IS NOBODY BEHIND YOU.

Aldo Capasso, Elisa Buiano, Carmen Terracciano, Sergio Di Petrillo, Vincenzo Materazzo, Claudio Pelosi (Naples, Italy)

Ilonch+vidalleARCHITECTURE: Fabian Llonch, Gisela Vidalle (New York, New York)

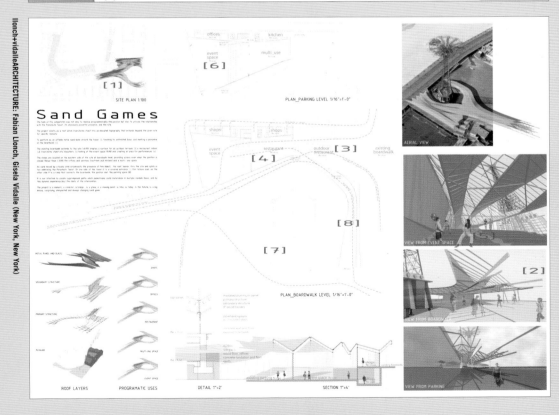

OK, WE ARE OUT THERE
BUT LOOK AT US !!!
THE REASON FOR THIS CHOICE

SCENIC TOWER PARACHUTE

Sand Games

Damon Rich, Anthony Titus (Brooklyn, New York)

Architecture of Fun — Architecture of Oppression

For the first half of the 20th century, Coney Island was celebrated for its modern architecture.

Over the following fifty years, it was stigmatized for the same reason.

Today, the rebirth of Coney Island requires a reconciliation between the two halves of its split modern personality: on one hand, the strange formal experiments of the Amusement District (the Parachute Jump most prominent among them), and on the other, the massive postwar housing blocks that form their architectural backdrop.

As a first step towards this reconciliation, we propose the Coney Island Kaleidoscope. The goal of the Coney Island Kaleidoscope is to reframe and remix the visual, programmatic, and formal elements of contemporary Coney Island.

While the utopian and futuristic flavor of towers in the park has been obscured by the idea of *the projects*, the Coney Island Kaleidoscope recaptures these serial forms at a miniature scale, using the technology of the carnival mirror to remix the surrounding architecture and reemphasize its exhilarating geometric abstraction.

Restaging the socialist dream of modern slabs at the beach, the plane of the boardwalk extends through the towers, canting up as it leaves the sea. The upper towers become a cluster of kiosks: food vendors, giftshops, exhibit spaces, and seating areas create the simultaneous pleasures of eating, people watching, shopping in one of the great landscapes of the 20th century. Below the plane, a double-height space houses interpretative exhibitions on the history of Coney Island and offices of community-based organizations.

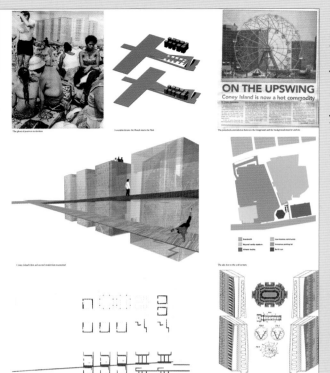

ON THE UPSWING
Coney Island is now a hot commodity

OA+Scap: Homero Hernandez, Juan Carlos Alvear, Horacio G. Merediz, Carlos Arce (Mexico City, Mexico)

THE PARACHUTE PAVILION
parallux
an open design competition for coney island

according to the ephemeral and mutant history of coney island, and the intention to regenerate the zone, we conclude that the pavilion must be a completely new symbol for the city.

this new landmark not necessarily have to be a second object competing against the Parachute structure.

the parachute itself could be re-evaluated.

then, the new pavilion is the revaluation and renovation of the old symbol.

the objective of the new structure is to illuminate and to emphasize the existing one, without even touching it. it works as a display cabinet. it works as a lamp.

the proposal creates a new urban circulation system which links the access points to coney island, and makes the people walk through the spaces of different heights among ramps that take them to every part of the program. First, in the ground level, the offices and the multi-use exhibition area are located, then some ramps raise around the Parachute structure and takes the user to the restaurant and the store, through ascending passages that functions as sky galleries as well as viewpoints.

the structure is a parallax object that by its geometry it is never perceived equal from its diverse angles.

"Parallux" is mutable like its own site.

plan (1" = 8')

section (1" = 8')

accesing points to the parachute pavilion

TALL buildings   0   30   60   90   120   150

Matthew Ford, Vasco Agnoli (Brooklyn, New York)

United States Barrage Balloon Corps

RECURITING CENTER
Proposal for the Coney Island Parachute Pavilion design competition
New York, 2005

Coney Island is Coney Island rises the Parachute Tower - a device for military training, converted from an amusement park ride. An age of expanded entertainment collides into the brutal realities of war fighting and the forward march of democracy. "America's Army," revealed and distributed by the US Armed Forces, becomes the most frequently downloaded online game. Dreamland becomes a weapon in the nation's war arsenal.

Amusement, entertainment and defense collide.

PAVILION PLAN

A Brief History

The Greatest Generation had what it took, and defeated the GREATEST EVIL EVER TO WALK THE EARTH. Above the Allied cities of England they spread barrage balloons. Pulling against gravity, they lifted cables that kept enemy aircraft from lower more effective bombing altitudes. And the mighty enemy fell.

New York City, 2005 - A blanket of balloons float above to defend the airspace and the American homeland below. In a time immediately after the manifestation of an AXIS OF EVIL, enemies arise around the world: Iraq, Iran, North Korea, Syria. WHEN ONE DOES NOT KNOW WHERE THE ENEMY IS, ONE MUST SPREAD A BLANKET OF PROTECTION, as a mother spreads a quilt over her slumbering infant. And the balloons rose.

Design Proposal

The Parachute Tower, a relic of a crazier amusement park era, meets the boardwalk and marks a place of new beginnings. A Recruiting Center for the U.S. Barrage Balloon Corps. The boardwalk, and the life that accompanies it, extends into the site. A stalwart billboard sign acts as a call to arms, attracting beachgoers and local residents to the Recruiting Center. A gondola, housing a Recruiting Office and Food Service Counter, is the heart of an open air pavilion.

Recruiting Office - The shining gondola floats below the sign with doors open. Volunteers, chosen from the ranks of the elite Corps, staff the Recruiting Office and recount their experiences to pavilion visitors who

clamor up to the counter. Paperwork and contracts are kept on hand for candidates to fill out. Across the pavilion exhibits are opened to display the exploits of the men and women of the USBBC.

Food Service Counter - Complimentary food is issued from the counter. Balloneers hand down prepared boxed meals to all comers. Cuisine from around the world is savored; a surprise in every box - Cous Cous, Sushi, Tandoori, Lasagna, Hot Dogs. A global cornucopia spills forth to the delight of small children, strapping youth and the elderly alike.

"It was my grandfather who first put words to the dreams I had seen in the history books. He had gotten a hot dog and signed the paperwork in between a round of skeeball and a ride on the bumper cars."

"I must have been 7 or 8 the first time I saw the balloons and really thought about them. We were at a family outing in Coney Island for a Cyclones game. A large sign stood behind the right field stands. I asked my Mom what it was and she said, "Son, that's the Balloon Corps. That's who makes all of this possible.."

"Once the balloons began repelling aerial invaders above the skies of New York City, their efficacy proven, they spread across the continent. Pittsburgh, Chicago, Detroit, St. Louis, Los Angeles. A nation rallied into the air."

- Floating Saviors: A History of the United States Barrage Balloon Corps

ARCHI-TYPE

A water cube, an expandable space, a modular system, a hanging garden, a rip curl, a bridgelike building. These projects re-envision the quintessential fairground pavilion as new architectural typologies.

P2: Tore Pape, Daniel Goldberg (Kassel, Germany, and London, United Kingdom)

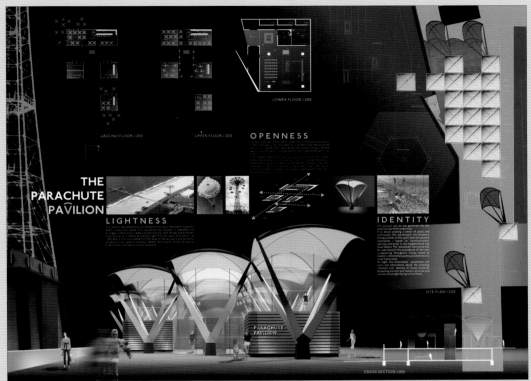

Marco Marcellini (Cos Cob, Connecticut)

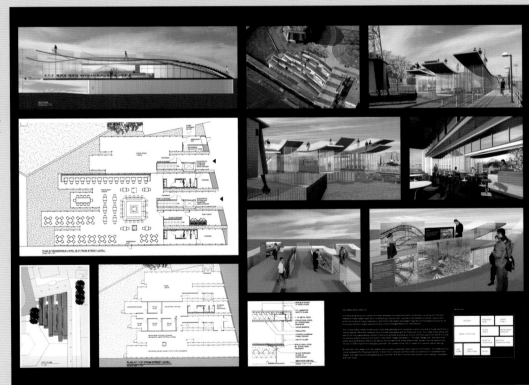

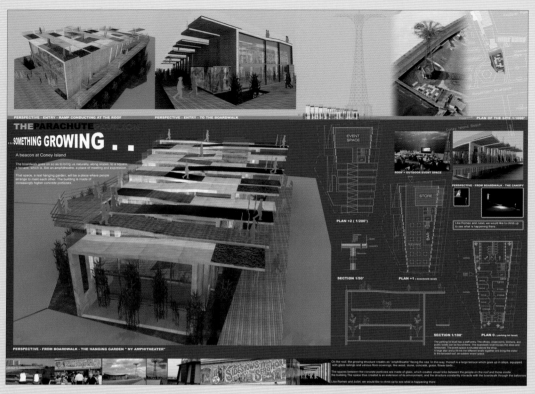

THE PARACHUTE
...SOMETHING GROWING . .

A beacon at Coney Island

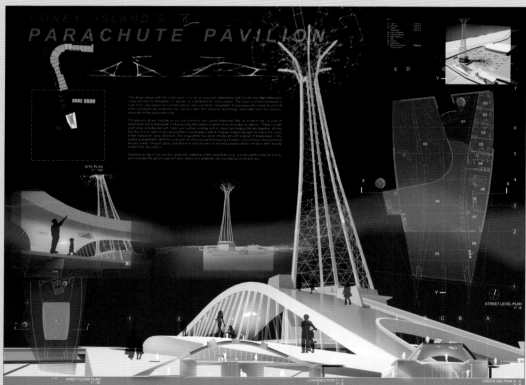

CONEY ISLAND'S
PARACHUTE PAVILION

2BMP: Nikita Bogachkin, Artem Melikyan, Anna Bogachkina, Sergey Panin (Moscow, Russia)

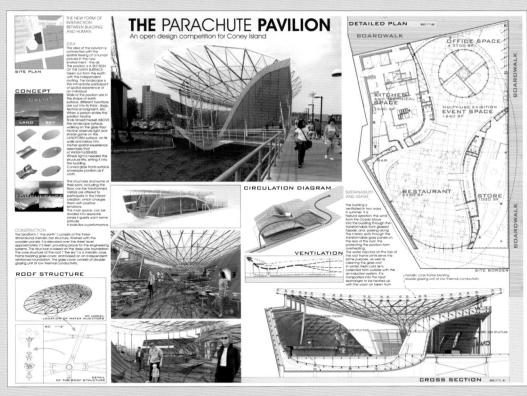

THE PARACHUTE PAVILION
An open design competition for Coney Island

SITE PLAN

THE NEW FORM OF INTERACTION BETWEEN BUILDING AND HUMAN

CONCEPT
CALM
LAND SKY
TURBULENCE

ROOF STRUCTURE
3D MODEL LOCATION OF WATER INJECTORS

DETAIL OF THE ROOF STRUCTURE

CIRCULATION DIAGRAM

VENTILATION

DETAILED PLAN
BOARDWALK
OFFICE SPACE
KITCHEN AND TECHNICAL SPACE
MULTY-USE EXIBITION EVENT SPACE
BAR
RESTAURANT
STORE
SITE BORDER

SUSTAINABILITY AND USAGE

CROSS SECTION

Evidence Design: Jonathan Pascarosa, Shari Pascarosa (Brooklyn, New York)

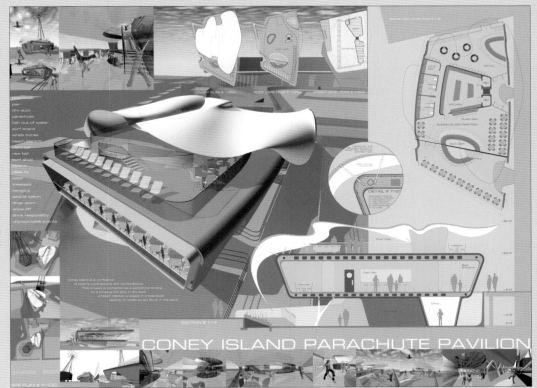

CONEY ISLAND PARACHUTE PAVILION

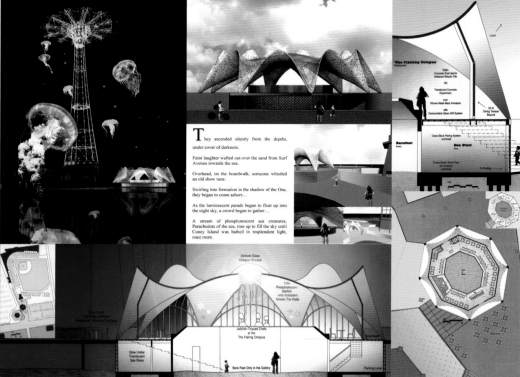

They ascended silently from the depths, under cover of darkness.

Faint laughter wafted out over the sand from Surf Avenue towards the sea.

Overhead, on the boardwalk, someone whistled an old show tune.

Swirling into formation in the shadow of the One, they began to come ashore…

As the luminescent parade began to float up into the night sky, a crowd began to gather…

A stream of phosphorescent sea creatures, Parachutists of the sea, rose up to fill the sky until Coney Island was bathed in resplendent light, once more.

PARACHUTE PAVILION

CONEY ISLAND . NEWYORK

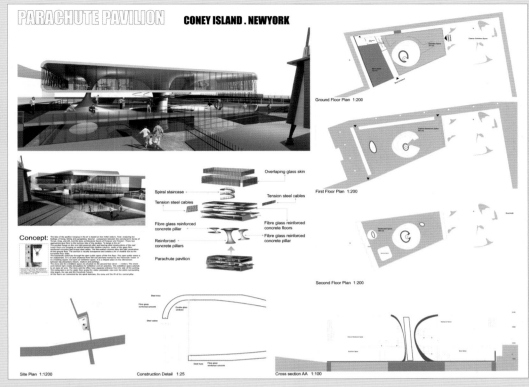

Ground Floor Plan 1:200

First Floor Plan 1:200

Second Floor Plan 1:200

Overlaping glass skin

Spiral staircase

Tension steel cables

Tension steel cables

Fibre glass reinforced concrete pillar

Fibre glass reinforced concrete floors

Reinforced concrete pillars

Fibre glass reinforced concrete pillar

Parachute pavilion

Concept:

Site Plan 1:1200

Construction Detail 1:25

Cross section AA 1:100

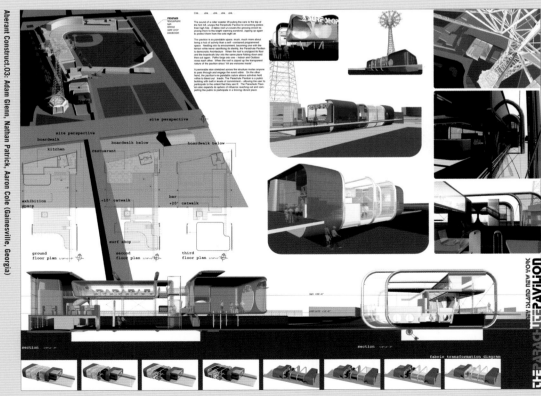

site perspective

boardwalk

kitchen

restuarant

boardwalk below

boardwalk below

exhibition space

+10' catwalk

bar

+20' catwalk

surf shop

ground floor plan

second floor plan

third floor plan

section

section

fabric transformation diagram

THE PARACHUTE PAVILION

CONEY ISLAND NEW YORK

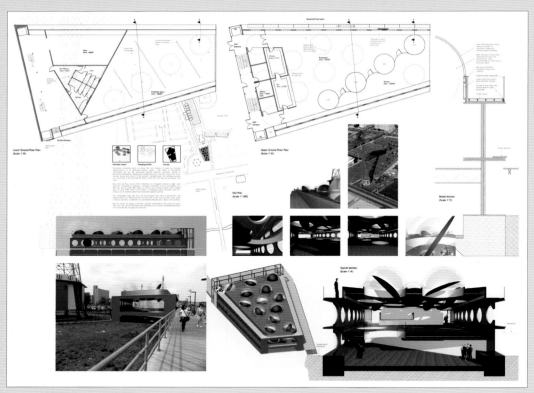

Koeppelund Fritz Architekten: Stephan Koeppel, Marianne Fritz (Munich, Germany)

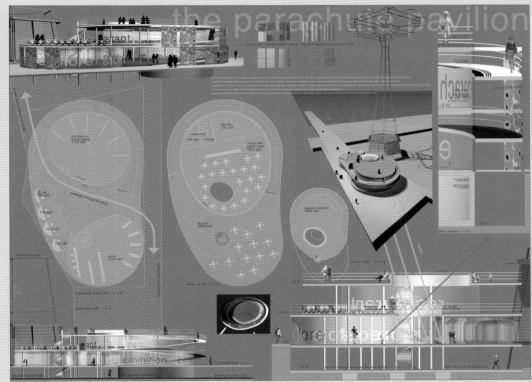

Thomas Lontine (Central, South Carolina)

WATER CUBE

THE WATER CUBE WOULD SERVE AS A LANDMARK MUCH LIKE THE PARACHUTE RIDE. THE WATER CUBE IS REMINISCENT OF THE OCEAN AND IS MUCH LIKE AN INFINITY EDGE SWIMMING POOL. THE WATER ORIGINATES FROM THE PIER AND CASCADES OVER THE GLASS WALLS. THE INTERIOR SPACE CAN BE VIEWED THROUGH THIS "WATER WALL," ENCOURAGING THE VISITOR TO EXPLORE THE INTERIOR. THE INTERIOR EMPHASIZES THE OPENESS OF THE VAST OCEAN. CEILING HIEGHTS ARE EXTREMELY HIGH AND MOST OF THE SPACES HAVE EXPOSURE TO THE WATER WALL. THE INTERIOR WALLS ARE INDEPENDENT OF THE CENTRAL PIER STRUCTURE. THERE IS A ONE FOOT SPACING ABOVE THESE WALLS WHICH IS FILLLED WITH GLASS TO EMPHASIZE THE DOMINANCE OF THE PIER STRUCTURE. THIS STRUCTURE MAKES A TWIST ON THE TYPICAL PIER; INSTEAD OF PUTTING THE FOCUS ON THE PIER ITSELF, THE FOCUS IS INSTEAD ON THE SPACES UNDERNEATH. THIS PIER HARKENS BACK TO THE PIERS OF THE OLD CONEY ISLAND. THE PIER CAN BE ACCESSED BY A STAIRWELL THAT EXTENDS THE EXHIBITION SPACE. AT NIGHT THE STRUCTURE SERVES AS A LUMINARY DRAWING THE ATTENTION OF PASSERBY.

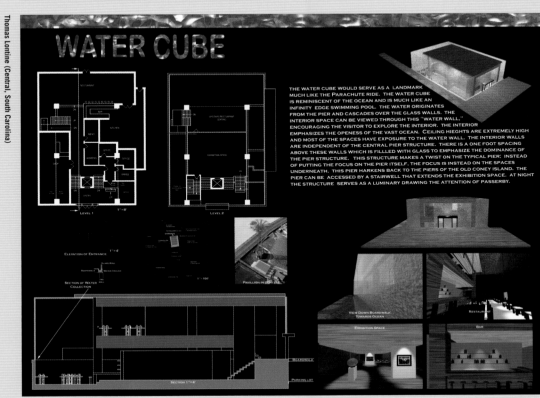

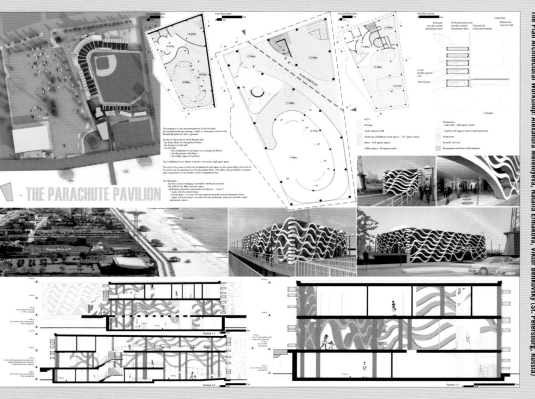

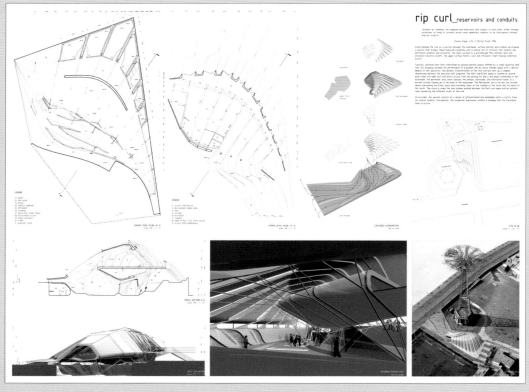

rip curl_reservoirs and conduits

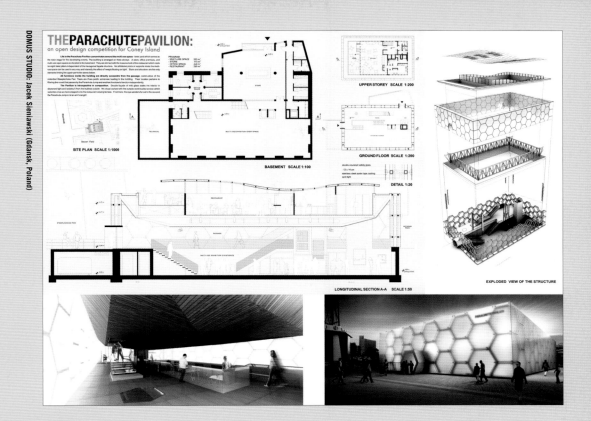

THE PARACHUTE PAVILION:
an open design competition for Coney Island

SITE PLAN SCALE 1:1000

BASEMENT SCALE 1:100

UPPER STOREY SCALE 1:200

GROUND FLOOR SCALE 1:200

DETAIL 1:20

LONGITUDINAL SECTION A-A SCALE 1:50

EXPLODED VIEW OF THE STRUCTURE

ACTIVE (S)PACE

These proposals not only push forward the idea of a pavilion as an activity generator, they are the event! Whether slow or fast paced, seasonal or year round, they are new recreational destinations.

Innovarchi Architects and Arup Engineers: Stephanie Smith (Innovarchi), Ken McBryde (Innovarchi), Alex Phegan (Innovarchi), Julien Vincent (Innovarchi), Tristram Carfrae (Arup Engineering) (Sydney, Australia)

GRAVITY park

AIR▷

Lara Gamant (Middletown, New Jersey)

Spray, Splish, Splash

Summer Fun in the Pool

Elegant Autumn Event

White Crystaline Bliss

Gliding on Winter Ice

Sprung Spring

Seasonal Surface

The history of Coney Island has always been directly tied to the water as a source of recreation. In this proposal, that connection is celebrated via a large multi-purpose surface extended from the boardwalk that is utilized year round as recreation in water's various stages. Besides serving a programmatic function, the surface also reflects the Parachute Jump and the dynamically changing sky. The rest of the program occurs below this surface with a view of the surrounding area through a screen of falling water or icicles, depending on the season.

Azevedo-Mayer-Kokotos: Asaf Mayer, Rubens Azevedo, Natalia Kokotos (London, United Kingdom)

Architcomplex: Daisuke Hirose, Hiroaki Imahashi, Tatsuo Katsumata, Naohiro Niinei, Yuji Uenosono (Tokyo, Japan)

THE PARACHUTE PAVILION

A new amusement in Coney Island:
It should be attractive and sustainable as a pavilion at the world famous seashore. A design aspect of highest priority is to pull in more people in to Coney Island in our proposal. It is for a competition game of inline skate, play field, restaurant, cafe and exhibition during all year long.

A main program:
16 feet and 12 feet vertical half-pipe ramp are on the roof for extreme sports, ex. skate board, inline skate and BMX. Many kinds of event will be opened within the extreme sports game and people will be able to enjoy another WAVE instead of sea wave and up-and down Parachute Jump. As those pipes have flat floor, named Deck, the roof will have options to be cafe and party lounge. On the roof, there are 3 platforms for game player and audience. They can see the sea, game and Parachute Jump from lookout point.

An architectural proposal:
The pavilion is built by precast concrete structure. Four concrete arches make line and they are connected by post tension cables. The idea of structure system is similar to highway construction. The section of pavilion is unique arch which generated by two ramp shapes and three reversed shapes. The pavilion has two floors, first floor and roof top. There are three separated tubes for cafe, restaurant and exhibition space which 20 feet height on the first floor. As the surface of pavilion is coated photocatalytic paint, the pavilion requires little maintenance for cleaning exterior.

Structural diagram

Ozge Gulec (Stillwater, Oklahoma)

THE PARACHUTE PAVILION- life of the boardwalk

Philippe Nolet, Sebastien Riendeau (Montreal, Canada)

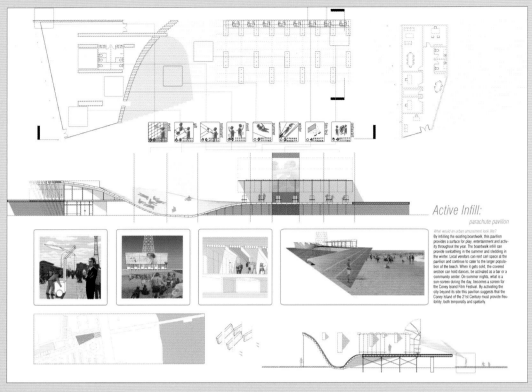

Active Infill:
parachute pavilion

What would an urban amusement look like?

By infilling the existing boardwalk, this pavilion provides a surface for play, entertainment and activity throughout the year. The boardwalk infill can provide sunbathing in the summer and sledding in the winter. Local vendors can rent cart space at the pavilion and continue to cater to the larger population of the beach. When it gets cold, the covered section can hold dances, be activated as a bar or a community center. On summer nights, what is a sun-screen during the day, becomes a screen for the Coney Island Film Festival. By activating the city beyond its site this pavilion suggests that the Coney Island of the 21st Century must provide flexibility, both temporally and spatially.

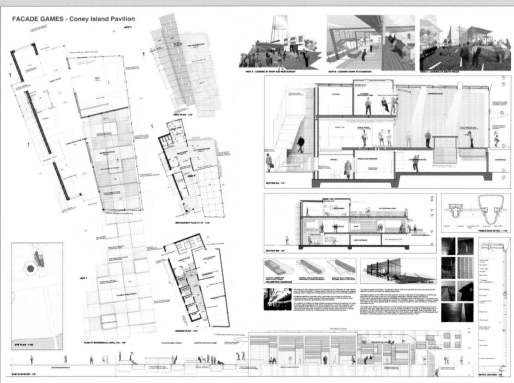

FACADE GAMES - Coney Island Pavilion

ROOF LEVEL 1" = 10'

BROADWALK LEVEL 1" =

PARKING LOT LEVEL 1" = 10'

SECTION AA 1" = 8'

KEYSPAN PARK

PERSPECTIVE LOOKING NORTH TOWARDS KEYSPAN PARK

PERSPECTIVE LOOKING SOUTH TOWARDS PARACHUTE JUMP

PERSPECTIVE LOOKING NORTH TOWARDS PARKING LOT

PERSPECTIVE LOOKING SOUTH TOWARDS PIER

DESIGN STATEMENT

PIAZZA - SOUTH WEST ELEVATION 1" = 8'

PIAZZA - NORTH EAST ELEVATION 1" = 8'

LEGEND

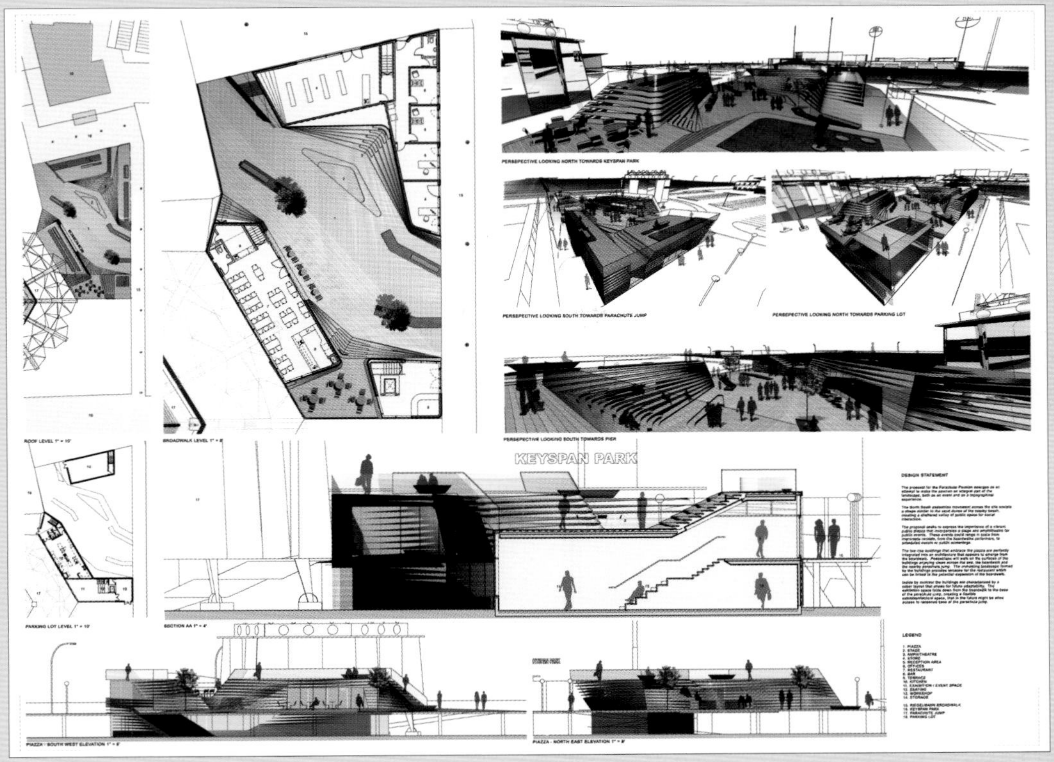

MEDIUM AS MEDIA

These pavilions are immersive environments. They act as media databases taking in and transmitting information in the form of advertising, videos, projections, and LED displays.

Remco Bruggink, Rob Hootsmans (Rotterdam, the Netherlands)

Milligram: Meredith Miller, James Dominic Graham (Princeton, New Jersey)

The Progenitor / Condenser :: A Documentary Pavilion

The parachute jump is an unintended vestige; the pavilion beneath it is its accompanying reliquary of the intangibles of the site. At the root of the pavilion is the accretion of place-data. Through the active recruitment of personal histories and recollections, an intensive documentation of site conditions, and a rigorously complete visual history, this narrative archive draws an ever-increasingly complete portrait of the place as it is and was. While the visceral sensations of the parachute jump can no longer be experienced, the pavilion will seek to describe it through the distillation of memory and image, recreating the sensations of the spectacle of Steeplechase Park.

Along with this non-artifactual archive, the site receives an infrastructural framework within which the fluidly adaptive commerce so endemic to Coney Island, can take place. Its structure utilizes the three main Coney Island typologies: surface-path, destination-spectacle, and the frictional zone of permeable storefront. It becomes an extension of the boardwalk, a surface to be occupied and extruded. The building is a frame, creating vistas and transparencies as well as defining zones of occupation.

The parachute jump itself, long functionless, is given a new task: a wireless internet transmitter is mounted to its apex, demarcating in its shadow this ephemeral pavilion, an area where place-data is fluidly received and broadcast. This flow of fact, image, and memory defines the site. Coney Island exists outside its material reality: it is a fuzzy and changing image propagated through photographs as well as individual memories, stories, songs.

Octagons: Monica Franklin, Aaron Vaden-Youmans, Marianna Mello (New York, New York)

UCA: Gibert Michael, Ohashi Manami (Tokyo, Japan)

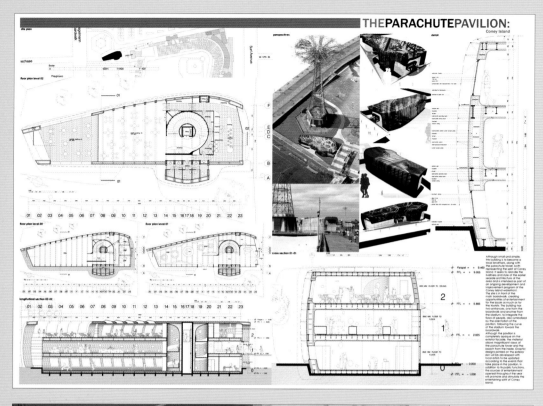

THE PARACHUTE PAVILION:
Coney Island

Pell Studio: Paul Kim, Matt Williamson, Ben Pell (Instructor) (Syracuse, New York)

HOLLOWgram
the (in)complete proposal for the Parachute Pavilion

Launchpad05—REDEK: Takuya Onishi, Chie Shimizu, Pornthep Chatpinyakoop, Sarapol Prukchartsiri, Bunpot Weeradacha (Bangkok, Thailand)

CONEY IRON NIKE Pavilion

Studio: Yinette Sanchez, Annelise Kouns (Miami, Florida)

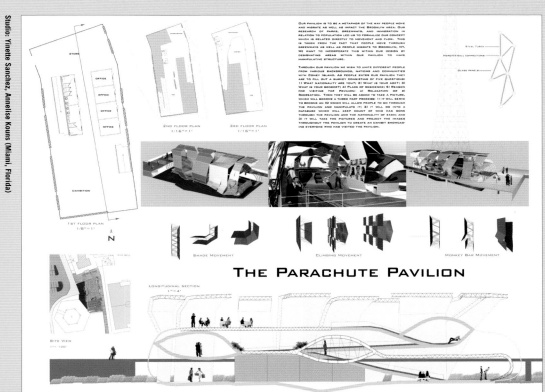

THE PARACHUTE PAVILION

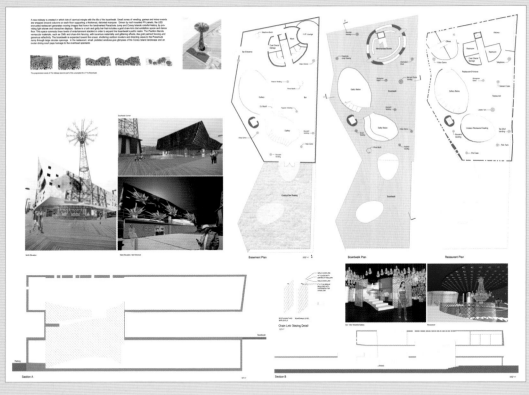

SteM: Marc Perrotta, Sofia Castricone, Teresa Ball (New York, New York)

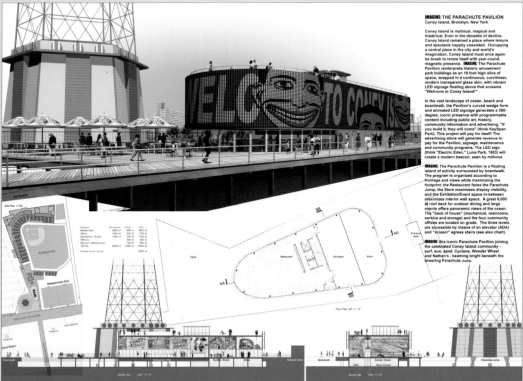

Frederic Schwartz Architects: Frederic Schwartz, Julia Murphy, Tomas Bauer, Jessica Jamroz, Gabriele Cavazzano (New York, New York)

IMAGINE: THE PARACHUTE PAVILION
Coney Island, Brooklyn, New York

Coney Island is mythical, magical and theatrical. Even in the decades of decline, Coney Island remained a place where leisure and spectacle happily coexisted. Occupying a central place in the city and world's imagination, Coney Island must once again be brash to renew itself with year-round, magnetic presence. **IMAGINE:** The Parachute Pavilion reinterprets historic amusement park buildings as an 18 foot high slice of space, wrapped in a continuous, curvilinear, modern transparent glass skin, with vibrant LED signage floating above that screams *"Welcome to Coney Island!"*

In the vast landscape of ocean, beach and boardwalk, the Pavilion's curved wedge form and animated LED signage generates a 360-degree, iconic presence with programmable content including public art, history, community information and advertising. "If you build it, they will come" (think KeySpan Park). This project will pay for itself! The advertising alone will generate revenue to pay for the Pavilion, signage, maintenance and community programs. The LED sign (think "Electric Eden," Luna Park, 1903) will create a modern beacon, seen by millions.

IMAGINE: The Parachute Pavilion is a floating island of activity surrounded by boardwalk. The program is organized according to frontage and views while maximizing the footprint: the Restaurant faces the Parachute Jump, the Store maximizes display visibility, and the Exhibition/Event space in-between maximizes interior wall space. A great 6,000 sf roof deck for outdoor dining and large events offers panoramic views of the ocean. The "back of house" (mechanical, restrooms, service and storage) and the four community offices are located on grade. The three levels are accessible by means of an elevator (ADA) and "scissor" egress stairs (see also chart).

IMAGINE: this iconic Parachute Pavilion joining the celebrated Coney Island community - surf, sun, sand, Cyclone, Wonder Wheel and Nathan's - beaming bright beneath the towering Parachute Jump.

Anton Kisselgoff, Karyn Lee (Brooklyn, New York)

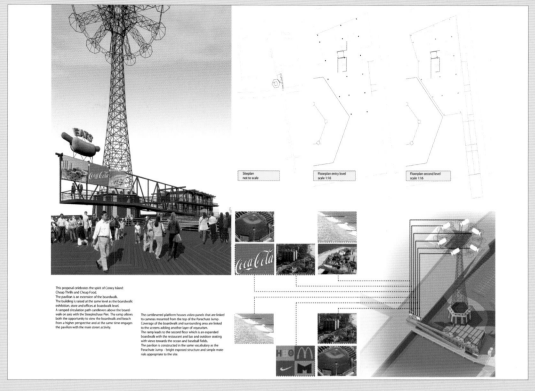

Siteplan
not to scale

Floorplan entry level
scale 1:16

Floorplan second level
scale 1:16

This proposal celebrates the spirit of Coney Island:
Cheap Thrills and Cheap Food.
The pavilion is an extension of the boardwalk.
The building is raised at the same level as the boardwalk:
exhibition, store and offices at boardwalk level.
A ramped circulation path cantilevers above the boardwalk on axis with the Steeplechase Pier. The ramp allows
both the opportunity to view the boardwalk and beach
from a higher perspective and at the same time engages
the pavilion with the main street activity.

The cantilevered platform houses video panels that are linked
to cameras mounted from the top of the Parachute Jump.
Coverage of the boardwalk and surrounding area are linked
to the screens adding another layer of voyeurism.
The ramp leads to the second floor which is an expanded
boardwalk with the restaurant and bar and outdoor seating
with views towards the ocean and baseball fields.
The pavilion is constructed in the same vocabulary as the
Parachute Jump – bright exposed structure and simple materials appropriate to the site.

Alexander Rodriguez, Alfredo Andia (Miami, Florida)

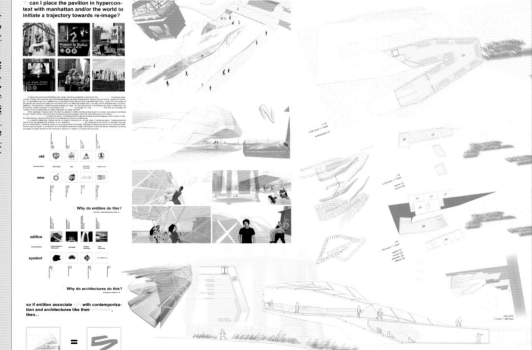

? can I place the pavilion in hypercon-
text with manhattan and/or the world to
initiate a trajectory towards re-image?

old

new

Why do entities do this?

edifice

symbol

Why do architectures do this?

so if entities associate ___ with contemporiza-
tion and architectures like their ___,
then...

TAKE AWAY

While very different from one another, these five projects provide essential items for the beach. These "organic and malleable" mats, "robotic reporters," beach chairs, branded water bottles, and goods dispensers disseminate a new identity for Coney Island.

Shift: Marc Hoppermann, Goetz Elmar Schrader (Vienna, Austria)

David Niemiec, Connar Walik, Jacklynn Arndt (State College, Pennsylvania)

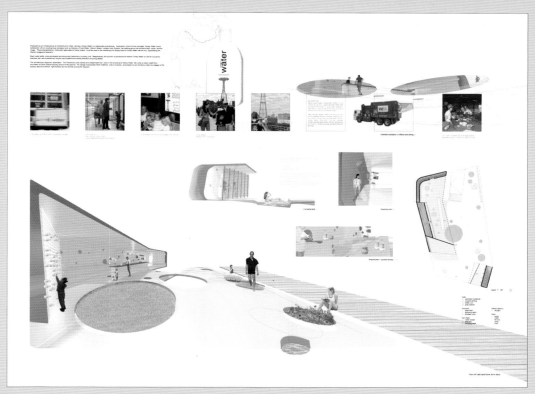

North Keeragool (Lubbock, Texas)

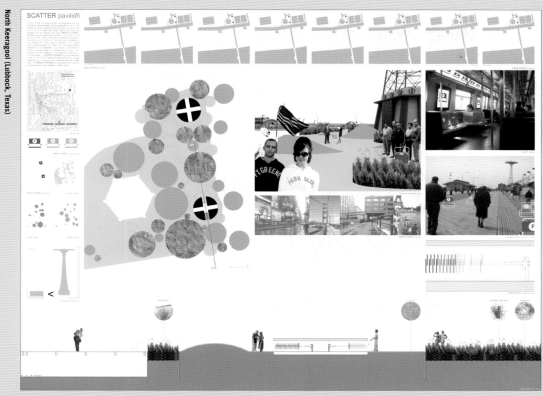

Matt Brown, Charles Mattern (New York, New York)

coneymat

coneymat

TAAN: Gundula Proksch, Florence Guiraud, Nancy Kim (Brooklyn, New York)

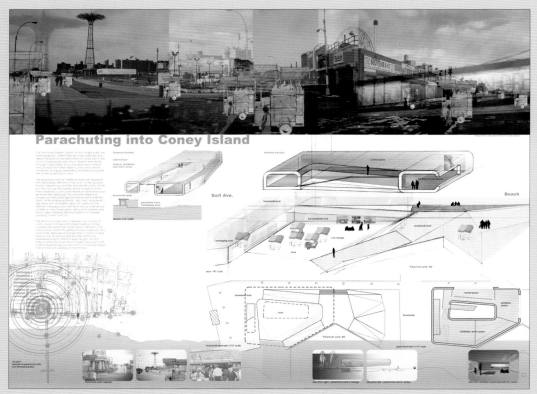

Parachuting into Coney Island

Surf Ave.

Beach

IV. THE VAN ALEN INSTITUTE
NEW YORK PRIZE

THE PAVILION: SYMBOL OF RECREATION AND REGENERATION
KEVIN CARMODY / ANDREW GROARKE / CHRIS HARDIE / LEWIS KINNEIR

The master plan being developed for Coney Island in New York seeks to reinvigorate this world-famous seaside resort. A key component of the plan is the Parachute Pavilion. Set against proposals for new commercial and retail developments and anchored beside the celebrated Parachute Jump, the new pavilion is intended as a symbol of regeneration and will provide an exhibition venue, restaurant, and public meeting place for tourists and local residents.

That the Parachute Pavilion has an inseparable relationship with its host, the seaside resort of Coney Island, prompted us to consider a design that would reflect the resort's physical, social, historical, and mythological context. The starting point for this research was an investigation into pavilions as markers for an event or function, who their tradition as recreational structures, and into their role as symbols or catalysts for urban regeneration.

As a London-based team working on a competition for a project overseas and as strangers to Brooklyn and Coney Island, we became interested in the fact that the typology of the pavilion is itself often considered as a "foreigner." The pavilion has historically had a transitory or indifferent relationship with its surroundings—for example, as a traveling marquee, an ornamental garden folly, or as a structure conceived for an exposition.

A Stage for Recreation

Pavilions are used as centers for meeting, entertaining, hosting special events, and retreats for physical and spiritual regeneration. Pavilions are seldom built out of a need for primary shelter. Rather, recreation and celebration have been the primary drivers for their being. For example, in war, pavilions were not built historically as battlements to defend one's territory but were constructed as places to celebrate and relax after a battle was won.

The painting *The Field of the Cloth of Gold* (ca. 1550), which celebrates the meeting between Francois I of France and Henry VIII of England, depicts a series of pavilions that serve various functions. There is the meeting place, named after the opulent cloth-of-gold coverings provided by the sovereigns and their entourages; the banqueting pavilion, in the foreground, houses the ceremonial dinner; the meeting of the monarchs occurs in a richly decorated tent, in the background; and a series of military tents decorated with heraldic emblems, scattered throughout the image, provides resting places for participants of the tournaments. Historically, pavilions have either represented extreme private wealth and decadence or symbolized a place for private retreat and meditation. Although the motive for creating a pavilion has shifted toward more public activities, their reason for being has remained the same: to attract attention and to provide visitors with a privileged place for contemplation.

The pavilion as a place of recreational activity has often provided an escape from the real world (not unlike the fairground). This was the case in the European garden pavilions of the eighteenth and early nineteenth centuries, which coquettishly decorated themselves in styles borrowed from architectural traditions and were often the venues for more decadent activity than society would countenance in more formal surroundings. Other examples, such as the pavilions designed for international world's fairs, were conceived as exhibition halls that condensed the culture of a nation into a singular theatrical temporary structure.

The garden pavilions of the eighteenth century were primarily reserved for use by the privileged and were built for the pursuit of leisure and social vanity. The pavilions were built as annexes to the main house or a place to decorate the gardens of the aristocracy and royalty. They were a reason for a promenade in the grounds to enjoy the view, a punctuation mark along a path providing brief shelter from the weather, a resting place for refreshments and conversation away from the strictures of court etiquette, or a strategic place to take a pause during the hunt and change horses. Without a pavilion, an eighteenth-century garden was not complete. As simple spaces, they examined the blurred interaction of nature and culture as a meeting space in the garden. Its interiors were almost incidental and served as a framing device for viewing both the landscape and the spectacle of social events, elaborating on the ideals of the picturesque.

The nineteenth century marked the end of pavilions as indulgent follies for private use only by affluent society and heralded the beginning of an era in which the pavilion became part of the public realm. Increasing economic strength afforded industrialized nations the opportunity to reward the middle and working classes with increased leisure time and an expendable income. This instigated new prototypical leisure activities for physical and cultural

Parachute Pavillion Site and Jump, Coney Island, 2005

The Field of the Cloth of Gold (artist unknown, attributed to Hans Holbein [1497–1543]), ca. 1550. Oil paint on canvas, 168.9 cm x 347.3 cm. Haunted Gallery at Hampton Court Palace, London. © 2006 The Royal Collection, Her Majesty Queen Elizabeth II

Herzog & de Meuron, EDEN Pavilion, Rheinfelden, Switzerland, 1987

Bathers in the breaking waves of the Atlantic Ocean, Coney Island, 1903

Luna Park at night, Coney Island, 1904

Shoot The Freak, Coney Island, 2004

gratification and a new genre of pavilions built as venues for recreation—amusement pavilions at the seaside and exhibition pavilions at the world expositions and fairs.

A Seaside Innovation

Seaside recreation was an invention of Victorian England born out of a belief in the health benefits of bathing. Quickly exported as a recreational activity for the masses to the rest of Europe and the United States, it was originally a pastime reserved for the more privileged and wealthier classes, who were also drawn by the seclusion from the city that the seaside offered.

Initially only the upper classes had the opportunity to use bathing pavilions, the accepted method of sea bathing at the time. The pavilions were drawn into the water by horses and provided both changing facilities and an enclosed bathing room for those able to afford it. These first bathing pavilions were rudimentary structures constructed in the interests of modesty, morality, and social acceptability. However, they became increasingly elaborate to conspicuously reinforce social standing and, as a result, became the backdrop to the spontaneous entertainment and the regimented performances of the affluent.

The first seaside resorts that flourished at this time to service sea bathing were increasingly driven by the growing demand for amenities, entertainment, and recreation. The introduction of leisure time for the workforce in the twentieth century—the advent of the annual vacation for the middle-class workforce—altered the general psyche of western society and further fuelled this demand for structured and paid recreation. As society became less interested in the notion of health and more attracted to the pursuit of pleasure. The morphology of the seaside resort reacted to this change.

Originally, a seaside resort occurred at the termination point of a single road running from a city to the sea. This route formed a processional path to the recreational activities, located where the road met the beach—a confluence of energy and activity. Pavilions, and piers, began to service the growing recreational trade or the resorts. The pavilions were the first expressions of economic development and recreational activity at the seaside. Amenities such as food and drink and entertainment soon followed, spurred by the economic possibility of the new tourist trade. Seaside towns flourished and local residents often became subservient to this seasonal opportunity for income.

Recreation increasingly became the focus of the seaside, and pavilions became the focus of the seaside resort. Small rotundas with brass bands, tents enclosing circuslike performances, and a variety of attractions in stalls lining

the boardwalk became the backdrop. Working throughout the day and night, the pavilions drew from a flamboyant palette of imagery and were often comprised of elaborate and theatrical lighting and decoratively painted facades. They aimed at creating a virtual utopia to which one escaped. The resort towns along the coastlines competed for the most unusual display of architecture and recreation, where the old was quickly dispensed with for next season's new. Like stage sets, these provisional structures created an exotic environment reminiscent of the fairground.

The mid-nineteenth century saw an increasing popularity of steam travel, and piers became landing stages for steamboats that ferried people from urban centers to the seaside resort. These landing platforms became an additional focus of activity on the beach. Around the entertainment pavilions located at the intersection of the pier and promenade was a bottleneck of frenetic activity and energy. The new pavilions constructed on the piers became even more fantastical structures hovering over the water. The collision between the manmade and the natural became the physical threshold for the seaside. The crossing of the pier became a mental release for the masses arriving at the seaside, symbolizing freedom from the everyday patterns of city life. The seaside was a new virtual reality that liberated visitors from the polite or urbane behavior enforced by city life.

The removal or suspension from the normal hierarchies and barriers in society encouraged an equality not found in everyday life. Previously objectionable rituals such as disrobing or bathing in public became acceptable, redefining notions of modesty and propriety. Amusement rides forced physical interaction in public, facilitating unlikely communication between people and fuelling the energy and frivolity of the environment. The pavilions became catalysts in breaking down physical and social barriers—the individual became unified with the crowd and inseparable from the environment of the seaside itself. The pavilions were the backdrops for the recreation but the spectacle was the audience itself.

An Instrument of Utopian Architectural Experiments

Paralleling the growing demand for recreation facilities at seaside resorts, the international world's fairs of the second half of the nineteenth century also became novel attractions for leisure and entertainment. The event structures that the fairs created became perhaps the most significant precursors to the modern pavilion. Beginning with the Paris Universal Exposition of 1867, they became a modern forum for the display of a nation's prosperity and status.

Expositions were a social experience as equally noble as visiting a gallery or museum while, at the same time, they invoked a sense of collective spectacle and pride.

The unprecedented popularity of the world's fairs, with each successive one trying to more accurately capture the zeitgeist than the one before, fuelled an energy toward creating exhibitions that were increasingly sophisticated and stimulating. The nature of these publicly funded, monumental events, which garnered international media exposure, generated a new, aggressively competitive architecture that had to achieve maximum effect with minimum means in a short time frame. Exposition fairs and their pavilion structures were commissioned, conceived, constructed, occupied, and dismantled or destroyed within a matter of months.

The unprecedented grand scale of these exhibitions required exceptionally magnificent gestures. For example, the Crystal Palace in London built in 1851 and the Palais du Champs de Mars constructed in 1867 in Paris placed great emphasis on a central representational structure. The commissions for these pavilions were awarded to heroic engineers (rather than architects) Joseph Paxton and Gustave Eiffel, respectively, as a way to commemorate the advances in a nation's technology through awe-inspiring structures. Their enormous glass palaces functioned as huge cultural and educational powerhouses sited in pleasant garden surroundings and containing a large number of other attractions.

In addition to the central pavilion, the ornamental grounds of the exhibitions were crowded with smaller structures whose task was to distil and represent aspects of their respective countries in miniature, making manifest the pavilion's subject matter in the architectural object itself. The skill and artistry of each nation was judged on its ability to capture, in a simple enclosure, the image of a fictional journey to that country—a fragment of its geography, history, or culture, offering the spectator a temporary displacement from his or her own origin. The fairs condensed a parody of the world into several acres of enclosed public space.

Despite their provisional nature, exhibitions consumed an unprecedented amount of resources because of their increasing enormity and created an entirely new approach to public space. Unlike previous fairs, markets, or carnivals, whose events invigorated existing urban spaces (streets, boulevards, and squares), these new colossal events were enacted on unprecedented scales so large that they required space that could not be found or could not be contained within the confines of the city—they had to be planned as satellites to it. The 1964 New York World's Fair,

dedicated to man's achievement on a shrinking globe in an expanding universe, was sited at Flushing Meadows Park in Queens, New York, and was the largest world's fair in the United States, covering over a square mile. The various pavilions of the fair clustered around a representational centerpiece, the Unisphere, with amusements, exhibitions, and visitor attractions. The IBM Pavilion, by Charles and Ray Eames and Eero Saarinen Associates, championed the information age within its ellipsoid-shaped theater through multimedia experiences, such as a series of films by the designers.

Unlike their contemporary counterpart, the seaside resort, world's fairs were often enclosed and had an entrance fee, differentiating between the upper and middle classes that were able to pay from the lower class that was not. This had a number of effects on the public space that the fairs created and how people behaved once inside. The security barriers and boundaries created an artificial city that paralleled a real city. Its role as a microcosm of a city liberated the architecture from any immediate physical, historical, or contextual meaning—the site of the world's fair therefore became contextless in terms of urban reference and subject matter. This deliberate and immersive environment disorientated and overwhelmed the visitors.

The amusement parks of Coney Island combined the success of the world's fairs and expositions to create a sense of escapism from everyday life. Dreamland, the third of Coney Island's main amusement parks, opened in 1904, was a corporate-motivated venture. Dreamland was the utopian model of an ideal city with amusements and attractions that condensed selected nations of the world into individual pavilions. Although mimicking the successes of its predecessor, Luna Park, Dreamland combined and referenced the neoclassical idea of the city explored in previous world's fairs.

Coney Island and the world's fairs were test beds for the ideal city. Their pavilions were the instruments of these utopian experiments. As Dutch architect Rem Koolhaas proposes in *Delirious New York: A Retroactive Manifesto for Manhattan*: "Coney Island is the incubator for Manhattan's incipient themes and infant mythology. The strategies and mechanisms that later shape Manhattan are tested in the laboratory of Coney Island."[1]

An Exhibition in Itself
The opportunity to create a pavilion is an irresistible assignment for architects and designers. Often without a program or the necessary regulations of a conventional building in its temporality, the pavilion has yielded some of the most adventurous and influential works of modern

architecture. Iconic examples include those from early modernists, such as Bruno Taut and Peter Behrens, to the canons of the modern movement, including Le Corbusier, Ludwig Mies van der Rohe and Alvar Aalto, to the great architects of the postwar period, the Smithsons and Charles and Ray Eames, to contemporary architects of international repute, such as Zaha Hadid, Daniel Libeskind, and Tadao Ando. Although pavilions continued to be designed as venues containing events and activities, the emphasis of the modern pavilion shifted from what is placed inside to the structure itself. For example, the only function that Mies van der Rohe's German National Pavilion for the 1929 Barcelona International Exhibition had to fulfil was to accommodate a reception for the King and Queen of Spain for the signing of the Golden Book, which marked the official opening of the exhibition. According to Mies van der Rohe, even the furniture designed and fabricated especially for the pavilion, such as the Barcelona chairs and stools, went unused during the opening ceremony. The experience of the space was, in fact, the exhibition. As architectural critic Martin Pawley writes: "No functional programme determined or even influenced its appearance. No part of its interior was taken up by exhibits: the building itself was the object on view and the 'exhibition' was an architectural space such as had never been seen."[2]

Unlike the other contributions that Germany made to the exhibition—installations for the various industries and an electricity supply station, which demonstratively boasted of advances in German technology—the pavilion presented itself as a symbol of the nation. Although dismantled in 1930 following the closure of the exhibition, it was rebuilt in 1986 on the same site to the original design and has since become a tourist destination.

The world's fairs and expositions instigated a legacy of the pavilion as architectural experiment. The Serpentine Pavilion, a temporary structure commissioned each summer by the Serpentine Gallery and installed in Hyde Park in London, is envisioned as a modern pavilion as architectural experiment. The building stands as the embodiment of the architect's concept rather than the activities that the pavilion hosts. As Julia Peyton Jones, director of the Serpentine Gallery confirms, the pavilions are meant to be read as "containers that need not contain." She continues that the pavilions are the most direct way of exhibiting the built manifestations of an architect's creative process: "The pavilion is a more bite-size, less intimidating way of experiencing architecture. The sense of public ownership is central to the success of the pavilions, the lack of public barriers and ticket sales reinforce this experience. People just wander in and out."[3]

Empty pavilion, Barcelona Pavilion, 2005

Alvaro Siza and Eduardo Souto de Moura, Serpentine Pavilion, London, England, 2003

Conceptual artists have also appropriated the pavilion as their medium. The installation pavilions by American artist Dan Graham epitomize this agility between maximum sculptural architectural container and minimum content. His installation for the 1976 Venice Biennale entitled *Public Space/Two Audiences*, is based on the biennale's theme of the architectural environment. In his supplemental text on the work he writes: "[it] was constructed to work in a specific container of 'Ambiente.' I wanted it to function doubly as art and as simply an exhibition pavilion (for itself), following the examples of Mies van der Rohe's Barcelona Pavilion or [El] Lissitzky's two exhibition rooms."[4]

Through the use of steel and glass, materials typically associated with commercial city buildings, Graham deliberately creates spaces that are formally austere. However, by creating his work at the human scale of a pavilion, he attempts to invert conventional associations and encourages the viewers to participate in the installation. Made from elemental pieces of mirrored glass, the pavilions further engage a visual exchange between the user, the object, and the context in which it is placed. Graham writes:

> The city, the suburb, the park, and nature are edged by four sides of glass. At the same time, his dematerialized, almost invisible panoptics—linking the inside to the outside in a permanently fluctuating geometry—are always associated with places beyond spaces, physical actual places, places that refer to a history, a memory, a community.[5]

Participants are literally suffused into the fabric of the pavilions, as is the landscape around them, in a continually changing kaleidoscope of images. The pavilions are unselfconscious meeting spaces for the observation of human behavior and for the exchange of views. The sense of permeability is central to their success. The lack of gates, doors, or barriers reinforces this experience. Like a bus shelter, people can just wander in and out at any time of day. Graham notes:

> Typologically, the work belongs to the park/garden's pleasure pavilion, which has been an antidote to the alienating qualities of the city as well as a utopian metaphor for a more pleasurable city in the future. These pavilions are used for people at restful play— a fun-house for children and a romantic retreat for adults. They are both emblematic of the power of the corporate city and help to dissolve the city's alienation effects. They also relate to the eighteenth century notion of the Arcadiona "rustic hut."[6]

An Embodiment of Event and Place

It is precisely because pavilions do not need to subscribe to conventional architectural rules and regulations—be weather tight, enduring, or pragmatic—that they are able to become experimental investigations into the built environment and embody an event or place. The pavilion to mark Bruges as the European Capital of Culture in 2002, designed by Japanese architect Toyo Ito, is analogous to Mies van der Rohe's Barcelona pavilion in that it was designed for a cultural event. However, rather than of representing the pride of a nation through its innovative design and use of new technology, Ito concentrated on creating a work that was site specific.

The pavilion's design references the historic context of the surrounding medieval buildings, such as the Town Hall. Its perforated structure made from an aluminum honeycomb mesh was conceived as a reference point to the tradition of lace-making in Bruges. At the same time, the intricate structure framed views of the city and encouraged visitors to look out into the urban environment. Although situated in the cobblestone Burg Square, the structure made reference to the waterways on which the city was founded. The rectangular box of the pavilion was built over the top of a shallow circular pool, situated where the Cathedral of St. Donatus had formerly stood two hundred years before.

Made from water, light, and metal, the transparency and simplicity of the pavilion provided a counterpoint to the city's history. Its translucent nature allowed for a constant play back and forth between the temporary installation and its enduring surroundings. For Ito, pavilions provide liberating opportunities for experimentation. Writing about the Serpentine Pavilion, another of his pavilion designs also realized in 2002, he notes:

> There is something very attractive about the idea of it existing only temporarily for three months. Whereas just the thought that the buildings I design might stand for a hundred years or more wears heavily on me, the notion of a temporary project is liberating in many ways. One need not be so strict about function nor worry about how it will age. And it seems to me, it just might offer the clearest expression of the concepts I habitually imagine.[7]

The Pavilion: A Symbol of Regeneration

Pavilions are inherently optimistic endeavors whether they are provisional or influential catalysts. They can often imply a necessary step forward by symbolizing an event or celebration or can be a token for the "shock-of-the-new." Their sudden imposition on a place or situation is often

Toyo Ito, Bruges Pavilion, Bruges, Belgium, 2006

Toyo Ito, Serpentine Pavilion, Hyde Park, London, England, 2003

Toyo Ito, Serpentine Pavilion (pavilion relocated), Battersea, London, England, 2004

Above and right: Niall McLaughlin, Bandstand, Bexhill-on-Sea, East Sussex, England, 2002

Rem Koolhaas, Serpentine Pavilion, London, England, July 2006

Charles and Ray Eames, IBM Pavilion, New York World's Fair,
Queens, New York, 1964–65

foreign to its immediate context and force fresh approaches to looking at the city and its spaces.

The relocation of Toyo Ito's Serpentine Pavilion, after its original exhibition in 2002, to the site of the derelict Battersea Power Station on the south bank of the River Thames does just this. Rather than operating as a garden pavilion as it was originally designed, it was dismantled and reassembled to stand now as a demonstrative symbol for the redevelopment of the neglected landmark.

Open to the public, Ito's pavilion is used as a marketing and information center for development plans and intended to be the conduit for local community project participation. Its temporary, slightly tentative occupation of an otherwise desolate site reinvigorates not only the riverside at this moment but also resuscitates the fabric of the pavilion itself for a second time. As prestige works the Serpentine pavilions are gaining the cache of artworks—either sold to anonymous private collectors or regenerated elsewhere to become the representational symbol of a new event. Koolhaas's latest addition to the Serpentine legacy has opened to the public in July 2006, and speculation is already mounting about its possible future incarnations once its hosting summer event has elapsed.

Aside from only a handful of other reconstructed examples from recent architectural history, the pavilion is typically destined to have a brief life, whose legacy is often consigned to an archive of architectural drawings, photography, and press articles preserving its memory in its pristine condition—as it was the day it opened.

Conclusion

Instinctively attracting attention to themselves, pavilions are catalysts for activity. As loci of public recreation, whether modest constructions containing amusements at the seaside, sophisticated architectural experiments at international exhibitions, artworks in the urban realm, or simple shelters, they can exist simply as an emblem or act more profoundly as a symbol of an event or place.

The etymology of "pavilion" can be traced back to its Latin origins—*papilio*, from which the word "butterfly" also stems. A literal comparison between the two derivations evokes connotations of brevity of lifespans, a fragile existence in which there is only transient inhabitation. With a defined sense of permanency, the pavilion must take on the form of a perpetual chrysalis. As a symbol of rebirth and regeneration, the pavilion must endeavor to propagate generation after generation of catalyzing activity by reappropriation of itself or its program.

Permanent or provisional, pavilions become embodied into the physical, historical, and cultural consciousness of a situation. Its typology has developed from an indulgent preserve of the privileged few to markers in the public realm that can inspire a collective experience. Whether a facilitator for public forums and events, or catalyst encouraging public participation in regenerating a neighborhood such as Coney Island, few other architectural typologies are able to court such attention by their simple spectacle. In its irreducible form, the pavilion is an attraction compelling interest in its beguiling and ambiguous definition—located in-between an idea and a permanent structure.

Notes

1   Rem Koolhaas, *Delirious New York: A Retroactive Manifesto for Manhattan* (New York: The Monacelli Press, 1978), 30.

2   Martin Pawley, *Mies van der Rohe* (New York: Simon and Schuster, 1970), 15.

3   Julia Peyton-Jones, *Fast-Forward Architecture: Serpentine Gallery Pavilion 2005* (London: Trolley Books, 2005).

4   Dan Graham, *Two-Way Mirror Power: Selected Writings by Dan Graham on His Art* (Cambridge, MA: The MIT Press, 1999), 155.

5   Dan Graham, quoted by Birgit Pelzer, *Survey: Dan Graham* (London: Phaidon, 2001), 66.

6   Graham, *Two-Way Mirror Power*, 175.

7   Toyo Ito, quoted by Julia Peyton-Jones, *Fast-Forward Architecture: Serpentine Gallery Pavilion 2005* (London: Trolley Books, 2005), 34.

V. COMPETITION ENTRIES

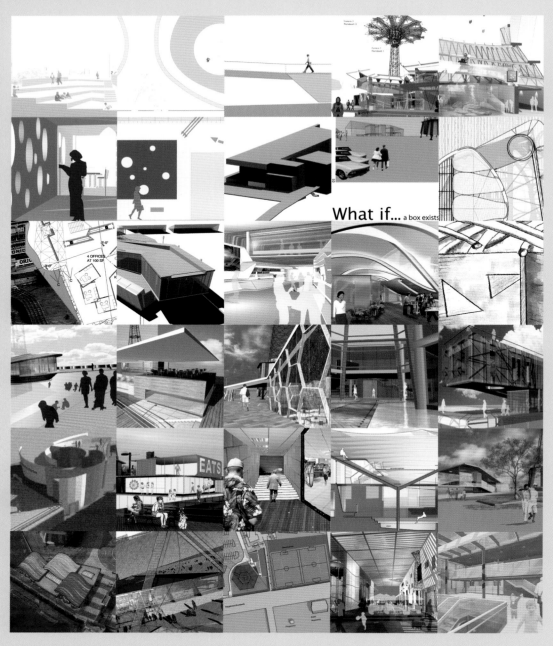

1. Wei Jien, Yee Jien (Brisbane, Australia) 2. Teruo Miyahara, Naomichi Kurata, Misa Horimoto, Fumitaka Takagi, Satoyo Yamamoto, Yukari Yamakoshi (Tokyo, Japan) 3. Ansgar Schmidt, Henning Ziepke, Ulrich Weingaertner, Kristina Gerdt, Annette Donat (Berlin, Germany) 4. Laura Foxman, Zach Riddley, John Romish (Portland, OR) 5. Neil Pelone, Wei Wei Shannon (Saratoga Springs, NY) 6. Brian Karlowicz, Rebecca Brannen (Atlanta, GA) 7.Yasuhiro Yamashita, Sato Jun, Kazuhiro Endoh Tokyo, Japan) 8. Laurence Garcia (San Antonio, TX) 9. Shadi Khadivi, Eleanor Lee, Esin Erez (Providence, RI) 10. Mike Hopper, Daniel Hoy (Eugene, OR) 11. Fortunato Luca Dettori, Martina Cozzolino, Dominique Ksol, Tiziana Falchi (London, United Kingdom) 12. Christopher Metz, Dan Piselli (Brooklyn, NY) 13. Steven Sanderson, Carmen Cham, Tyler Goss, Garrett Belmont, James Black (New York, NY) 14. Chi Ying Shen, Brian Kornreich, Sandy Mercado, Jacob Slutsky, Zachary Kostura (Brooklyn, NY) 15. Kate-Issima Francin, Leyna Owen (Boynton Beach, FL) 16. Yaniv Josef (Buckinghamshire, United Kingdom) 17. Lucio Muniain, Rodrigo de la Mora, Paola Morales, Marielle Rivero, Alfonso Patarroyo (Mexico City, Mexico) 18. Tony Leung (Hong Kong, Hong Kong SAR) 19. Maria Bermudez (Queretaro, Mexico) 20. Brian Stump (Anchorage, AK) 21. Marcello Della Monica, Gaetano Gravagnuolo (Vietri sul Mare, Italy) 22. Kailin Gregga, Steven Lazen (New York, NY) 23. Darrell Westcott (Lubbock, TX) 24. Popular Architecture with Formactiv: Casey Mack, Ron Eng, Eugenie Huang (New York, NY) 25. Nan Zhou, Yu Wen (Chicago, IL) 26. Earl C. Mayuga, Henry Mayuga (Vancouver, Canada) 27. Charisse Bennett (Stillwater, OK) 28. Marco Bozzola, Giovanni Cavallazzi Torres, Fabio Gatti (Novara, Italy) 29. Ateliers O, Maxime Pion, Guillaume Credoz, Souraya Haddad (Richelieu, Canada) 30. Richard Alomar, Byoung Lee, Karey David (New York, NY)

1. Frank Ryan, Mark Putney, Nina Stiber (Madison, CT) 2. Speranza Octavia, Mary Michal O'Dell (Brooklyn, NY) 3. Erick Ascencio, Ena Motley (Bronx, NY)
4. David Barr, Tyler Swanson (San Francisco, CA) 5. Mick Haley, Aaron Fletcher, William McGuinness, Audrey Lematte, Samuel Price (London, United Kingdom)
6. Philip Ryan (Brooklyn, NY) 7. SLLB Architects, Ltd: Daniel Smith, Tori Thames, Raj Patel, Andrius Gedgaudas, Seki Hirano (London, United Kingdom)
8. Sarah Holstedt (Stillwater, OK) 9. Nathan Carter (Stillwater, OK) 10. De Leon Primmer Architecture Workshop: Roberto de Leon Jr., M. Ross Primmer (Charlotte, NC)
11. 42D Architecture: Richard Bednarczyk, Terry Durden (Bloomfield, NJ) 12. John Houser (Lubbock, TX) 13. Patrick Stremler, Ulrich Gradenegger (Karlsruhe,
Germany) 14. Matteo Belfiore, Roberto Tranchese (Napoli, Italy) 15. Geo. Knipp (Kansas City, MO) 16. Michael Piper, Tim Sliger (Atlanta, GA) 17. Mauro Delgrosso,
Daniel Nadal, Juan Javier Pirez (Montevideo, Uruguay) 18. Yvonne Su, Yan Zheng, Bryan Wren (Arlington, TX) 19. Frank Garcia, Sergio Perez (Miami, FL)
20. Steven Clarke, Steven Herzberg (New York, NY) 21. Eungsoo Kim, Jeongyoun Cho, Nubras Samayeen (New York, NY) 22. Thomas Mercier, (San Luis Obispo, CA)
23. Randy Williams (Lubbock, TX) 24. Gregory Sobotka, Gretchen Stoecker (Venice, CA) 25. Misela Gonzales (Lubbock, TX) 26. Priscila Jimenez, (Weston, FL)
27. Rafael Cazorla, Mary Kate Wood (San Francisco, CA) 28. Melissa Weese (Marseille, France) 29. Michele Cetera, Rocco Cetera, Lea Cetera, Xenia Diente,
Steven Ng (Staten Island, NY) 30. Stephen Mueller, Keith Van de Riet (Brooklyn, NY)

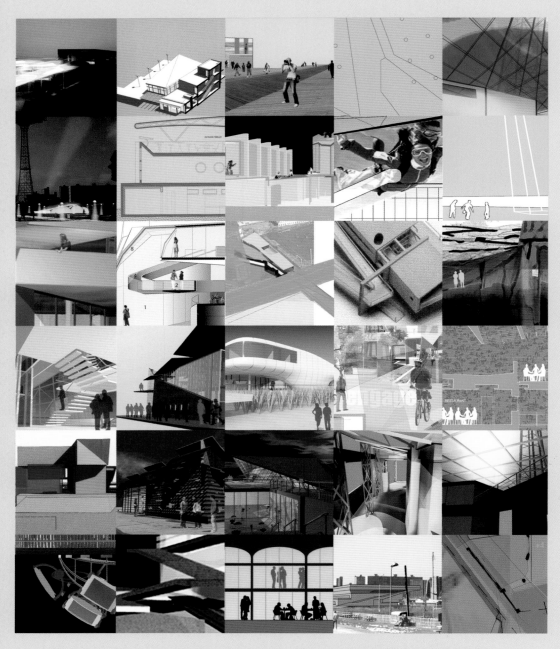

1. Drop Four: Andrew Vann, Kevin Hirth, Thomas Kelley, Christopher Donnelly (Charlottesville, VA) 2. Graham Clegg, Kristin Hopkins (Cambridge, MA)
3. Andy Summers, Ulrika Eriksson (London, United Kingdom) 4. Joshua Eckert (Stonewall, TX) 5. Alex Nussbaumer, Luis Casiano, Tim Sudweeks, Chris Thomas,
CarloMaria Ciampoli (New York, NY) 6. Lynn Przywara, Crystal Schenk (Philadelphia, PA) 7. Eduardo del Valle, Mariano Alemany, Hasit Panchal, Mark Schreiber
(Newark, NJ) 8. Kerry Barrett, Kertis Weatherby (Syracuse, NY) 9. Pei Lun Lin (Sunnyside, NY) 10. Antoine Cloutier-Belisle, Martin Champagne (Montreal, Canada)
11. Julien Paulre, Alexandre Becker, Paul Pflughaupt (Paris, France) 12. Gresley Abas Architects: Ahmad Abas, Philip Gresley (Perth, Australia) 13. Jenny Tse,
John Thurtle (Los Angeles, CA) 14. Jason Chandler (Coral Gables, FL) 15. Sandra Callejas, Melissa Elliott, Maria Arellano, Joy Wang, Daniel Silverman (Alexandria,
VA) 16. Gizem Erkaya, Tugba Ozbay (Ankara, Turkey) 17. LG2R: Amy Finley, Daniel Guich, Susan Reid, Jessica Rubin (Chicago, IL, USA) 18. Baerlecken + Reitz:
Judith Reitz, Daniel Baerlecken (London, United Kingdom) 19. Epodic Rhizome, Tavin Yeiter, Zach Benedict (Bluffton, IN) 20. K Martin Kristensen (Toronto, Canada)
21. Justin Huang, Rueytsu Huang (Berkeley, CA) 22. Anshuman Raje, Nikhil Kamat (Los Angeles, CA) 23. Trinity: Jeroen Semeijn, Ruben Groot, Femke Bakker
(Delft, the Netherlands) 24. Travis Harrison (Mountain Rest, SC) 25. Wilbur Sharpe (Myrtle Beach, SC) 26. Ezra Wittner, Amanda (Mandy) Davis, Aika-Grace Temu,
Matthew Collins, Ezra Wittner, JC Woodall (High Point, NC) 27. Diana Visentin, Nathalie Ospina (Doral, FL) 28. Christoph Schmidt, Matthias Lorenz, Susan Vecsey,
Jonas Schmidt (Basel, Switzerland) 29. Hans Herrmann, Matthew Warner (Brooklyn, NY) 30. Diane Fellows (Oxford, OH)

1. Kenneth Powley (Edmonton, Canada) 2. David Ostinga (Sydney, Australia) 3. Jeff Temple (Culver City, CA) 4. Erica Spicer (Lubbock, TX) 5. Daniel Takahashi (Lubbock, TX) 6. Alec Zebrowski (Middletown, CT) 7. Austin Millspaugh (Lubbock, TX) 8. Michael Laviano (New York, NY) 9. Alberto Nicolau (Madrid, Spain) 10. Xander Vermeulen Windsant, Cindy Wouters, Joost Koerver (Delft, the Netherlands) 11. Pedro Yglesias de Oliveira, Maria Ana Castro Caldas, Rita Abreu, Antonio Cassiano Neves (Lisbon, Portugal) 12. Richard McGrew (Las Vegas, NV) 13. Chelsea Sekula (Lubbock, TX) 14. Antonio di Oronzo, Jose Adames, Hoi Chen, Timothy Kim Park (New York, NY) 15. Meltem Anay, Hakan Anay, Ulku Ozten (Ankara, Turkey) 16. Thomas Loftus, Darryl Cook, Min Yoo, Kevin Keating (New Rochelle, NY) 17. Scott Utter (Chicago, IL) 18. Jaffer Kolb (Middletown, CT) 19. Jennifer Ho (Montreal, Canada) 20. Jackson Blalock (Clemson, SC) 21. Richard Healey-Finlay, Wolfgang Ripberger, Kristina Bird (Sydney, Australia) 22. Pu Chen (Jersey City, NJ) 23. James Kirkpatrick (Toronto, Canada) 24. Petar Mattioni, Toygar Targutay, Serena Chen (Plainsboro, NJ) 25. Ama Design Studio: Pedro Maia, Raul Pinto (Aveiro, Portugal) 26. Wesley McElhany (Lubbock, TX) 27. Michael Stewart (Brooklyn, NY) 28. Jedidiah Weeks (Stillwater, OK) 29. Dave Wellspring (Oxford, OH) 30. Karen Hock, Sven Schroeter (New York, NY)

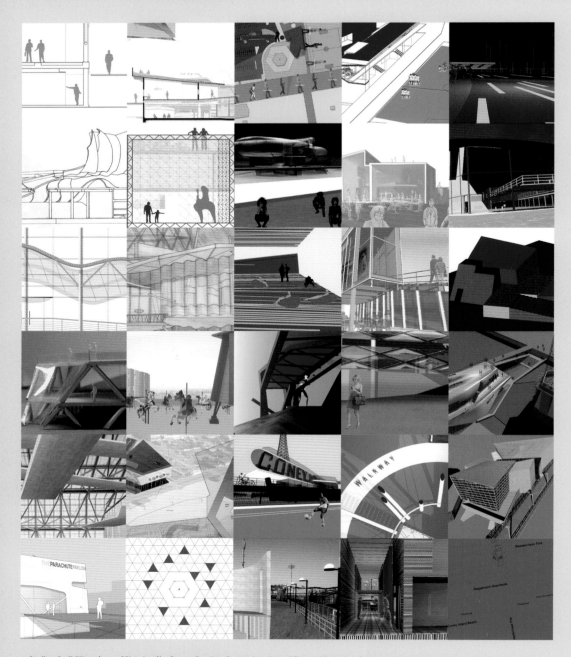

1. Geoffrey Graff (Westminster, CO) 2. Jennifer Gurney, Daughtry Carstarphen, Henry Miller, Ani Schaeffer (Brooklyn, NY) 3. Agatino Rizzo, Nunzia Gabriella Chisari (Nicolosi, Italy) 4. Sonia Leimer, Susan Kraupp (Vienna, Austria) 5. Zhe Wang, Fei Dai (Austin, TX) 6. Davin Hoyt (Lubbock, TX) 7. Helene Boyer, Cynthia Carbonneau, David Clavey (Longueuil, Canada) 8. Nilufer Kozikoglu, Fulya Akipek, Kayi Akipek, Ersin Temurcan (Istanbul, Turkey) 9. Michael Droob, Mads Pedersen, Peter Gamborg (Copenhagen, Denmark) 10. Travis Pawley (Edmond, OK) 11. Pablo Roquero (Montevideo, Uruguay) 12. Joseph Mazzitelli, Helen Obuchowicz (Toronto, Canada) 13. Cristina Balet Sala, Monica Sedano Peralta, Elisa Leoni, Manuela Parolo (Milano, Italy) 14. Sebastian Bieganowski, Jakub Rozmuski (Warsaw, Poland) 15. Daniel Alvarado Jr. (Lubbock, TX) 16. Anda Greeney (Middletown, CT) 17. Nikolay Nedev, Peter Nedev, Elizabeth Cardona, Cristina Canton (Cambridge, MA) 18. Gustavo Slovik, Enrique Pinzon, Alan Bonder, Harumi Martinez, Juan Pablo Ojeda (Mexico City, Mexico) 19. Adam Kekula, David Pulkrabek (Prague, Czech Republic) 20. Chia-Hung Wang, Cheng-Chiang Chung (Taipei, Taiwan) 21. Filemon Aragon (Lubbock, TX) 22. Emulsion Architecture: Yen-Yen Teh, Nerma Cridge, Neil Sharman (London, United Kingdom) 23. Ian Shao, Scott Kadlec (Chicago, IL) 24. Mitchell Chan (Ottawa, Canada) 25. Cezary Pruszkowski (Brooklyn, NY) 26. Markus Fiegl Architekt: Markus Fiegl (Berlin, Germany) 27. Albert Cuso, Albert Brufau (Barcelona, Spain) 28. SiAe Sung, Austin Sakong, Micah Jude Nickerson (New York, NY) 29. Studio Tomevski: Tome Tomevski, Vladimir Tomevski (Helsinki, Finland) 30. Francheska Barreto, Cory Mitchel (Marietta, GA)

1. Esther Kardos (Brooklyn, NY) 2. Johan Tonsgard, Monika Pitura, Ignacio Gonzalez Galan, Alvaro Martin Fidalgo, Petra Thedin (Rotterdam, the Netherlands) 3. Yeon-Cheon Na (Mount Prospect, IL) 4. Laura Heim, Nathalie Borne (Paris, France) 5. Neal Thomson (Ann Arbor, MI) 6. Gronli & Christensen: Sindre Gronli, Vilhelm Christensen, (Oslo, Norway) 7. Cottalorda Julien, Peres Mireille (Remire Montjoly, French Guiana) 8. Boguslaw Witkowski (TPD & A—Witkowski), Marek Morawski (TPD & A—Witkowski), Tim Thornton (Ove Arup / engineering), Barney Jordan (Ove Arup / engineering), Luc Wijnhoven (Kitchen Technology), (Braine l'Alleud, Belgium) 9. David Wiborg (Newton, MA) 10. David Magid, Maggie Peng (Brooklyn, NY) 11. Tomasz Bona, Dariusz Bona, Elzbieta Chylinska (Wood Ridge, NJ) 12. CheNitta Givens (Lubbock, TX) 13. Charles Lathan (Clemson, SC) 14. Christine Caine (Cambridge, MA) 15. Miguel Martinez, Scott Crawford (Jacksonville, FL) 16. Jason Spanier (Allston, MA) 17. Razvan Iliescu, Cristina Iliescu, Mihai Antoniu, Bogdan Ioncea, Andrei Gorea (Bucharest, Romania) 18. Penny Loukakou, Tzina Sotiropoulou (Athens, Greece) 19. Timothy Onderdonk, Grace Colby-Pancir (Wading River, NY) 20. Trouchon Eymeric (Langeac, France) 21. Irena Hradecka, Jan Svec (Prague, Czech Republic) 22. Jesperi Vara (Helsinki, Finland) 23. Scott Lukens, Ben Rantilla, Azure Logsdon, Brandilyn Fry, Josh Haney, Rosy Harris (Akron, OH) 24. Billy Harris (Norman, OK) 25. William Haggard, Oliver Klimpel (London, United Kingdom) 26. Krissy Weik, Anna Kolak, Dan Caruso, Keith Weik (Chicago, IL) 27. Wolfram Uanschou, Reinhard Wohlschlager, Georg Hofmann (Vienna, Austria) 28. James Dowling, Shannon Dowling (Los Angeles, CA) 29. Monika Kowalska (Chicago, IL) 30. Jerome Scott, Robert Kristof, Carrie Morrison, Dan Boyne (Columbus, ND)

1. Simon de Ruijter, Niels van Veen, Vincent Nowee (Delft, the Netherlands) 2. Justin Kyle (Lubbock, TX) 3. Bradley Horn, Maria Berman (New York, NY)
4. Ramiz Sonmez, F. Neyran Turan (Cambridge, MA) 5. Mandi Hoskins, Robert Ernst, Mark Siwek (Seattle, WA) 6. Vitaly Ganopolsky, Mark Jurcic, Adrian Dias (New York, NY) 7. Joseph King (Chicago, IL) 8. Hundredhands: Bijoy Ramachandran (Bangalore, India) 9. Norbert Jokiel, Andres Ginestet, Marco Heinsdorf, Paul Bungarten (Dusseldorf, Germany) 10. Joshua Weiselberg, Selin Semaan, Julian Tepper (New York, NY) 11. Jose Domingues, Ana Sofia Lopes (Braga, Portugal)
12. Amani Rizk, Martine Laprise (Montreal, Canada) 13. Robert Matelski, Lisa Tilder (Instructor) (Columbus, OH) 14. Jessica Caruthers (Lancaster, PA)
15. Hamilton Hadden, Hale Everets (New York, NY) 16. Toshiya Kogawa (London, United Kingdom) 17. Katherine Bubriski, Jeffrey Keilman (Albany, NY)
18. PK Thistle Architecture: Michael Thistle, Kevin Thistle (Henderson, NV) 19. Ctrl_Substance: Campbell Garratt, Benny Tang, Chris Ziegler, Matthew Hilyard (New York, NY) 20. McLain Clutter, Joaquin Bonifaz (New York, NY) 21. Andre Krammer, Bettina Buettner (Vienna, Austria) 22. Ahmed Youssef (Nutley, NJ)
23. Jorge Barrero (Brookfield, IL) 24. Mark Schimmenti, Dave Kenny, Patrick Hazari, Amy Robertson, Brian Ambroziac, Katherine Ambroziac (Knoxville, TN)
25. Bealmaus: Maurizio Scalera, Benedetta Alessi, Ranelagh (Dublin, Ireland) 26. Michal Stys, Rafal Specylak-Skrzypecki (Warsaw, Poland) 27. Lauren Ross, Elizabeth Easterling (Blacksburg, VA) 28. Viraline: James Vira, Margaret Gardiner Vira (New York, NY) 29. Michael Perez (North Miami, FL)
30. Carlos Garijo Vidal, Carmen Mazaira Castro (Madrid, Spain)

1. John Peek, Ben Regnier (New York, NY) 2. William Coleman (Clemson, SC) 3. Jaron Lubin, Olin McKenzie (Cambridge, MA) 4. Judith Carolin Mees (Middle Village, NY) 5. Odile Compagnon, Jim Lasko, Rebekah Alderson, Marylou Ibadlit, Camille Yu (Chicago, IL) 6. Fabrice Bonnardel, Frederic Bruneau, Thibaud de Brisoult (Lyon, France) 7. Wing Wong, Judy Cheng (Washington, DC) 8. Ruben Santos (San Francisco, CA) 9. Michael O'Boyle, Tracy Smith (Santa Monica, CA) 10. Steven Mankouche, Danielle Pato, Mark Davis (Birmingham, MI) 11. Aaron Moncibaiz (Lubbock, TX) 12. Gwo-Shenq Wey, Jia-Yuan Cheng, Tsing-Lan Lillian Yang, Chun-Ming Lee, Daniel Yao (Rego Park, NY) 13. Robin Blodgett, Jay Gorman (Brooklyn, NY) 14. Luciano Basauri, Dafne Berc (Zagreb, Croatia) 15. Alexander Waesch, Thilo Jennewein (Stuttgart, Germany) 16. Kyle Bunke, Brian Rezentes, Lisa Tilder (Instructor) (Columbus, OH) 17. Houman Sharif, Ghazaleh Jamei (Tiburon, CA) 18. Dana Cupkova-Myers, Martin Myers (Schroon Lake, NY) 19. SWBR Architects & Engineers: Kathleen Kaminski, Heather Flannery, Robert Simonetti, Todd Bruce, Olivia Bruce, Iain Tait (Rochester, NY) 20. Murat Soygenis, Sema Soygenis, Ertugrul Morcol, Togan Tong, Yasemin Yilmaz, Erdal Aydin (Istanbul, Turkey) 21. George Cooper, Ryan Kovalak (New York, NY) 22. Kiho Choi, Kwang Pyo (Steve) Koh (Washington, DC) 23. Joseph Jattuso, Stacey Jattuso (Brooklyn, NY) 24. Nicole Boyer (Oxford, OH) 25. Stacy Cahill, Jane Wernick (London, United Kingdom) 26. Daniel Glazer (Cambridge, MA) 27. Diego Carvajal, German Espitia (Brooklyn, NY) 28. Liang Hou (Brussels, Belgium) 29. Richard Heger, Veronika Bartosova (Prague, Czech Republic) 30. Jeffrey McKean, Annalisa Menozzi, Matteo Tanzi (New York, NY)

1. Mariano Sagasta, Joslyn Oppenheimer (Rotterdam, the Netherlands) 2. Vivian Wang, Peter Coombe, Jennifer Sage, Kit Yan, Joanne Liou, Ben Koenig (New York, NY) 3. Brian Rex (Lubbock, TX) 4. Roberto Caddeo, Giuseppe Ruscica (Mogliano Venetotreviso, Italy) 5. Daniel Spore (Evanston, IL) 6. Alex Chen (Vancouver, Canada) 7. Xavier Ortiz (Barcelona, Spain) 8. Sai Yan Chu (Oxford, OH) 9. Christoph Burkhardt, Markus Mueller, Volker Zepter (Stuttgart, Germany) 10. Peter Eichberger, Christina Lunzer, Robert Voeroes (Vienna, Austria) 11. Victor Gwiazda, Marion Gwiazda, Alina Jakubowska, Michael Poplawski (Munich, Germany) 12. Jakub Sztur, Bodo Juelicher, Alexander Haerter (Aachen, Germany) 13. Lucie Boyce Flather (Cambridge, MA) 14. Alexandra Merten, Gerlad Kappelmann (Hamburg, Germany) 15. Alan Power (London, United Kingdom) 16. Chungho Min (Chicago, IL) 17. Jason Foster, Bryan Thomas (Brooklyn, NY) 18. Joseph Enciso (Lubbock, TX) 19. Marcello Ferri, Stefano Ferrari (New York, NY) 20. Emanuel De Sousa, Joo Rainha Castro (Oporto, Portugal) 21. John Lin, Deane Simpson, Ida Richter Braendstrup (Sheung Wan, Hong Kong) 22. Jayyun Jung, Joonsang Park (Jersey City, NJ) 23. Sebastien Garon, Julie Tran (Ottawa, Canada) 24. Roberto Sforza, Alessandro Sforza, Benedetto Montalbano, Andrea Peruzzi (Rome, Italy) 25. Lucas Lau (Melbourne, Australia) 26. Richard Robbins, Jorge Yara (Islip, NY) 27. Jamie Jeffs, Vladimir Radutny (Chicago, IL) 28. Theo Kelaiditis, George Bizios (Toronto, Canada) 29. Yosuke Kawai (Oxford, OH) 30. Danilo Bogdanovic (Dusseldorf, Germany)

1. Andrew Maynard, CJ Koay, Matt McClurg (North Melbourne, Australia) 2. Alejandro Crudo (Buenos Aires, Argentina) 3. James Bruno, Patricia Oliveira (Farmingdale, NY) 4. Nicholas Banks (Lubbock, TX) 5. Murray Gilmour (Vancouver, Canada) 6. Andrew Balden (Lubbock, TX) 7. Junya Nakatsugawa, John-Eric Chung (New York, NY) 8. Kirsten Tudor (Garland, TX) 9. Christoph Falkner, Rainer Froehlich, Thomas Grasl, Georg Unterhohenwarter, Simon Zoppoth (Vienna, Austria) 10. Ebami Tom, Pieter van der Pot (The Hague, the Netherlands) 11. Michael Gilbert, Nicholas McWhirter (Grand Prairie, TX) 12. Katie Moore (Lubbock, TX) 13. Cinzia Abbate, Carlo Vigevano, Toyohiko Yamaguchi, Bruno Masci, Giovanni Betti (Rome, Italy) 14. Mary Caroline Eskridge (Greenville, SC) 15. Pedro Vieira (Figueira da Foz, Portugal) 16. Anna Erica Delai (Milan, Italy) 17. Andrew Santa Lucia, Olivier Montfort (Miami, FL) 18. Douglas Eaddy (Scranton, SC) 19. Kohki Hiranuma (Osaka, Japan) 20. Robin Anezin, Fabrice Andry (Paris, France) 21. Pragati Goswami, Praza D' Zouza, Manju Jayawardana, Vikram Grewal (Top Ryde, Australia) 22. Phil Peterson, Christoph Sauter (Berlin, Germany) 23. Michael Bade (Oxford, OH) 24. Teodoro Cambeiro, Tamara Abramzon (Brooklyn, NY) 25. David Rooth (Amherst, NY) 26. Claudio Ronconi, Andrea Spiccallunto, Danilo Dominioni, Michele Coletti, Stefano Chiaromonte, Michele Chiaromonte (Perugia, Italy) 27. Jed Laver (Lubbock, TX) 28. Eduardo Herrera, Leonardo Riano (Miami, FL) 29. Zaklina Gligorijevic, Milos Velimirovic, Nenad Novakov (Belgrade, Serbia and Montenegro) 30. Miguel Lacasta, Marc Chalamanch, Carmen Santana, Francesc Planas, Patrick Lau, Nikulaus Steinke, Jasmin Gomez, Christine Koelmel, Gerrit Fluthwedel (Barcelona, Spain)

1. Marcus Carter, Kim Yap (Brooklyn, NY) 2. Sanaz Shirshekar (Montreal, Canada) 3. Daniel Mintz (Jerusalem, Israel) 4. Nicholas Roberts (Glasgow, United Kingdom) 5. Philip S. Black (Ottawa, Canada) 6. Peter Macapia, Jae Hong Lee, Ashley Henley, Margaret Kirk, Joe Didio, Antonio De Angelis, Daisuke Hirose, Adam Guttenplan, Sam Krevor (New York, NY) 7. Hon Kong Chee (London, United Kingdom) 8. Tom Maul, Robert Hutchison, Candy Wang (Seattle, WA) 9. Jason Clark (Norman, OK) 10. Andrew Schuster, Tony Schonhardt, Carl Sterner (Cincinnati, OH) 11. Jimmy Sinis, Christopher Kallinosis (Pembroke Pines, FL) 12. Andrea Caputo, Matteo Sacchetti, Joana Rodrigues, Beatrice De Carli (Milan, Italy) 13. John Lenti (Chicago, IL) 14. Jim Howeth, Nate Neergaard (Bozeman, MT) 15. Derek Ham, Nyirabu Nyrabu (Hampton, VA) 16. Byron Terrell, Rahman Polk (Chicago, IL) 17.Gertjan Nijhoff, Petra Gerrits (Rotterdam, The Netherlands) 18. Brock Danner (Nutley, NJ) 19. Hong Joo Kim (Cambridge, MA) 20. Patrick Head, Brian Melcher (New York, NY) 21. Gideon Danilowitz, Jarod Allen (Venice, CA) 22. Jarret Hudson (Clemson, SC) 23. Chandler Growald (North Richland Hills, TX) 24. Nick McCormick, Dallas Huard, Bronwen Harms, Brad Kahler (Bozeman, MT) 25. Elissa Masin (Rockville Centre, NY) 26. John Jackson III, Nisa Janek (Muncie, IN) 27. Peter Meacock, Trevor Eastell, Simon Hurst, Matthew Wilkins, Paul Goddard (Bristol, United Kingdom) 28. John Hilgeman (Melrose, MA) 29. Gerard de Gorter, Melle Pama, Peter van Lier, Markus Hudert (Hoofddorp, the Netherlands) 30. Vasco de Mello, Rodrigo de Mello, Arthur Delgado da Costa, Renata C. Calfat, Vanessa Q. Fernandes (Sao Paulo, Brazil)

1. Kohei Kashimoto, Mari Matsumoto (Osaka, Japan) 2. Takao Akagawa, Koki Matsushita, Kana Murakami (Kitakyushu, Japan) 3. Jerzy Elzanowski, Andre Savoie (Montreal, Canada) 4. Shin Noguchi, Ryota Higaki, Tomoyuki Kurokawa, Masashi Suzuki, Kaoru Hagimori (Nishinomiya, Japan) 5. Jared Simon, Troy Leyva (New York, NY) 6. Chad Cornette, Paul Deleeuw (De Pere, WI) 7. Eddy Joaquim (San Francisco, CA) 8. Mitja Kosir, Ina Pravica (Ljubljana, Slovenia) 9. Kok Loong Wong (London, United Kingdom) 10. Joshua Van Donge, Kristina Kesler (Seattle, WA) 11. Daloh Designs: David Lohmeier, Nancy Herman-Thompson, Chuck Franklin, Matt Gilligan (Newport News, VA) 12. Shift Design: Brian Hsia, Katalina Arboleda, Nicholas Hollot, Diane Sit (Philadelphia, PA) 13. Gary Stoltz, Grainne Cassidy (Chicago, IL) 14. Jan Schevers, Jan Kuijpers, Dick van Lieshout (Eindhoven, the Netherlands) 15. Anthony Cricchio, Ronnie Parsons, Thomas Feuerstein (Arlington, TX) 16. Michael Sharir, Nick Musser, Andrew Allwine (Philadelphia, PA) 17. Wei Shan Chia, Elisabeth Ruinard (Sheffield, United Kingdom) 18. Joseph Tai (Hong Kong) 19. Neil Thelen (Ann Arbor, MI) 20. Robert Gaddy (Florence, SC) 21. Jose Bernal, Alfredo Andia (Miami, FL) 22. Ole Smith, Pernille Bisgaard, Harpa Heimisdottir, Rolf Nielsen, Peter Gram (London, United Kingdom) 23. William Cooper (Lubbock, TX) 24. Tom Guglielmo, Claudia Wolf, Johann Senner (Ueberlingen, Germany) 25. Christoph Wassmann, Ute Bauer (Vienna, Austria) 26. John Szot (Brooklyn, NY) 27. Sunggoo Yang (Cambridge, MA) 28. Gail Peter Borden (Raleigh, NC) 29. Gaetano Fazio (Forest Hills, NY) 30. Dan O'Riley (Chicago, IL)

1. Ryoji Karube, Andrea Day (Brooklyn, NY) 2. Mario Kuibus, Claudiu Bica, Tudor Vasiliu, Alex Axinte, Valentin Varlan (Bucharest, Romania) 3. Woohyun Park (Oxford, OH) 4. Min Suh (Hoboken, NJ) 5. Robert Redford (London, United Kingdom) 6. Fabio Valenza, Angela Campagna (Castellana Grotte, Italy) 7. Christian Nicolas (Rotterdam, the Netherlands) 8. Sara Grant, R D Gentzler (New York, NY) 9. Elizabeth Ward, Emily White (Brooklyn, NY) 10. Khoi Tran (Amsterdam, the Netherlands) 11. Cynthia Markhoff, Oskars Redbergs, Juergen Scholte Wassink (Frankfurt, Germany) 12. Kate Thatcher, Stephen Nielson (New York, NY) 13. Maria Derevencova, Martin Gallovsky, (Paris, France) 14. Christopher Kupski (Brooklyn, NY) 15. Ryan Cain, Katelyn Gardner, Eric Smith, Ryan Dirksen (New York, NY) 16. Jack L. Gordon Architects: Jack Gordon, John Ingram, Jonathan Silverman, Matthew Toomajian, Andrew Jones (New York, NY) 17. Marc Manack, Mark Supelak, Lisa Tilder (Instructor) (Columbus, OH) 18. Adam Golinczak (Brooklyn, NY) 19. DaeSun Park, YoonSuk Kang (Chicago, IL) 20. Brant Long, Glenn Hajadi (New Albany, OH) 21. Michael Delgado (Lubbock, TX) 22. Anthony Dong, Queenie Tong, Samson Oshirunde (Brooklyn, NY) 23. Chun Cheng Kuo, Szu-Yuan Tsai (San-Chung City, Taiwan) 24. Francois St-Hilaire (Montreal, Canada) 25. Allen Beedy, Heather Roether, Lisa Tilder (Instructor) (Columbus, OH) 26. Kevin Sperry, Asako Sperry (Brooklyn, NY) 27. Tristan d'Estree Sterk (Chicago, IL) 28. Andrew Parli (Stillwater, OK) 29. Matthew P. Greer (Union City, NJ) 30. Adam Sokol, Esin Yurekli (New York, NY)

1. Jyana Messenger, Alex Broadbent (Layton, UT) 2. Shawn Casey, Gina Cornman, Marlon Heywood (Boynton Beach, FL) 3. Chris Gerrick, Misun Chung (Seattle, WA) 4. Noe Munoz (Lubbock, TX) 5. A-Square, Inc.: Christopher Teeter, James Pereira, Andrew Thompson, Marty Klain (New York, NY) 6. Amanda Higley (Oxford, OH) 7. Katrine Bidstrup (Copenhagen, Denmark) 8. Andrea Fiechter, Alexandra Kern (Zurich, Switzerland) 9. Nishant Lall (Cambridge, MA) 10. Hong Il Kim, Jae Heon Shim, Kyung Ran Kim (Seoul, Korea) 11. Manuel Lodi, Paola Pilotto, Danilo Cupioli, Silvia Rizzo, Antonio Bergamasco (Genoa, Italy) 12. Jelena Mitrovic, Jelena Perovic, Tanja Gavrilovic, Tatjana Miladinovic, Radmila Nikolas (Belgrade, Serbia and Montenegro) 13. Cary Tomas Bellaflor, Aaron Zeligs, Matthew Tompkins (Corona, CA) 14. Harry Lowd, David Constable, Jessica Leete, Brian Rebain, Jacob Ward (Mill Valley, CA,) 15. Andy Ku, Kam Ku (Los Angeles, CA) 16. Peter Vatkov (Concord, CA) 17. Michael Tom, Adam Alder, Catherine Burns, Kyoung Min Seo (Brooklyn, NY) 18. Cesare Monti, Stefania Shaw (Chivasso, Italy) 19. Talal Rahmeh, Anas Younes (Damascus, Syria) 20. Carmine Raimo (Pompei, Italy) 21. Jari Paukkonen (Espoo, Finland) 22. Alexandra Heese, Cary Siress (Zurich, Switzerland) 23. Jay Stoughtenger (Cambridge, MA) 24. Carter Leung, Paul Davison (Emeryville, CA) 25. Jeff Nesbit (Lubbock, TX) 26. Jack Green, Marianne Jorgensen (Bristol, United Kingdom) 27. Lynne Opper, Christopher Dufresne (Great Barrington, MA) 28. Margot Krasojevic (London, United Kingdom) 29. Michelangelo Zaffignani, Rene Bechter (Feldkirch, Austria) 30. Vera Cirilo, Marco Mateus (Costa De Blanes-Mallorca, Spain)

1. Zac Monro (London, United Kingdom) 2. Follett-Iglesias Molli Arquitectos: Nick Follett, Fernando Iglesias Molli, Guillermo Carosella, Sebastian Schioppa (Buenos Aires, Argentina) 3. Jerome McInnish (Smyrna, ID) 4. Chiu-Fai Can, Daniela Mauro (San Donato Milanese, Italy) 5. Giorgio Ceradelli (Torino, Italy) 6. Joseph Karadin (Forest Hills, NY) 7. Maki Hashizume, Ei Ishiyama Yuichi Kawashima, Yusuke Nakayama Aiko Yamamoto, Takako Ikuta (Osaka, Japan) 8. Brian Johnson (Brooklyn, NY) 9. Waldemar Piasecki (Doha, Qatar) 10. Kerim Demirkan (Brooklyn, NY) 11. Pell Studio: Chrissy Arnold, Tessa Fleck, Ben Pell (Instructor) (Syracuse, NY) 12. Pekka Pakkanen, Risto Huttunen, Santeri Lipasti (Helsinki, Finland) 13. Gerald Pde, Habari Warjri (Jersey City, NJ) 14. Sebastien Riss (Paris, France) 15. Hannah Moon (Florence, TX) 16. Emanuel Kambanis, Namsoo Kim, Martha Kyriakidou, Andrew Kambanis (Astoria, NY) 17. Nishan Kazazian, Peter Mathias, Hans Gesell (New York, NY) 18. Mary Sterling Watkins (York, United Kingdom) 19. Okke-Jan Boom, Jorn Reijnders (Eindhoven, The Netherlands) 20. Stefano Gianani (Brescia, Italy) 21. Phil Kallsen (Seattle, WA) 22. Raffaele Razzano, Tom O'Connor, Peter Halkias (Westbury, NY) 23. Leung Cheuk Fo (Hong Kong, Hong Kong SAR) 24. Brandon Benjamin (Clemson, SC) 25. Florian Pfeifer (Vienna, Austria) 26. YI Works: Taewook Lah, Sungwon Yoon (Weehawken, NJ) 27. Jochen Kraske (Munich, Germany) 28. Raul Wallaart (Leiden, The Netherlands) 29. Alexander Haeusler, Silvia Benedito (New York, NY) 30. Patrick Lenssen (The Hague, the Netherlands)

1. Gregory Giroux, David Lavoie, Laurence Cote-Leclerc, Guillaume Belisle (Quebec, Canada) 2. Joanna Pamula, Krystian Gagis (Seattle, WA) 3. Sung Kim (Alexandria, VA) 4. Nicholas Gilliland, Imke Plinta (Paris, France) 5. John Blanchard, Chris Bosse (Sydney, Australia) 6. Marino Fionda (Cassino, Italy) 7. Ralph Ferme (Fenton, MI) 8. Christopher Penndorf (New Rochelle, NY) 9. Josean Ruiz Esquiroz, Ignacio Ruiz Allen (Madrid, Spain) 10. Tunch Gungor (Cambridge, MA) 11. Nicole Thame (Miami, FL) 12. Michael Payne, Mark Raggett (Portland, OR) 13. Willeke Smit, Annika Hermann (Amsterdam, the Netherlands) 14. Richard Sarrach, Tamaki Uchikawa (Brooklyn, NY) 15. Hans-Georg Baum (Ulm, Germany) 16. Kumiko Hayashi (Yokohama, Japan) 17. Regan Holton (Stillwater, OK) 18. Vijay Mohan, Raman Nagaraja (Chicago, IL) 19. Corey Sosebee, Ben McCreary, Steve Hudgins (Blacksburg, VA) 20. Antonio Lupoli, Andrea Lupoli (Naples, Italy) 21. Olaf Jasnorzewski (Tarnow, Poland) 22. Philip Tusa, Philomena Marano (New York, NY) 23. Amy Force (Lubbock, TX) 24. Sonya Kharas, Asher Israelow (Middletown, CT) 25. Annie Saunders (Clemson, SC) 26. Taylor Currell (Lubbock, TX) 27. Jongkyu Lee (Stillwater, OK) 28. Andrew Meckfessel (Lewisville, TX) 29. Pericle Gheorghias, Rodrigo Guajardo (Sunnyside, NY) 30. Ismo Rellman (Tampere, Finland)

1. Katherine Dankberg (Encinitas, CA) 2. Grupo MVD: Diego Stetskamp, Carolina Cossaro (Guadalajara, Mexico) 3. Osamu Morishita, Go Inagaki, Hiroshi Watanabe, Namika Nakamura (Osaka, Japan) 4. Andre Soluri, Fiona Cousins, Ricardo M. Pittella, Anaele Owunwanne (New York, NY) 5. Kneeling Bus: James Pfeiffer (Brooklyn, NY) 6. Jose Reyes, Roberto Miatello (Uniondale, NY) 7. Tirumala Rao Kootikuppala (Hyderabad, India) 8. Frank Cunha III (Ridgefield, NJ) 9. Chris Nikkel (Stillwater, OK) 10. Allison Torpey, Owen Detlor (Middletown, CT) 11. Carla Carenzo, Nicoletta Carbotti (Torino, Italy) 12. Antti Mykra (Helsinki, Finland) 13. Luis Oscar Osio Grasso, Claudia V. Espinoza Fregoso, Fco. Leobardo Ruiz Casillas, Jose Domingo Uriarte Parra (Guanajuato, Mexico) 14. Angelyn Chandler, George Kroenert (Jackson Heights, NY) 15. Erikjan Vermeulen (Amsterdam, the Netherlands) 16. Riley Triggs, Jonathan Smith (Austin, TX) 17. Sang Lee, Se Jung Kim, Brian N. Kim, Sae-Hyun Kim (Providence, RI) 18. Jean Francois Colyn (Charleroi, Belgium) 19. Abul Fazal Mahmudun Nobi (Dhaka, Bangladesh) 20. Sean McCormack, Andrew Karlson, Vincent Filigenzi (Chicago, IL) 21. William T. Baird Jr. (Brooklyn, NY) 22. Jeff Klancer (Valparaiso, IN) 23. Brinn Sustala (Lubbock, TX) 24. Hector de la Pena (Mexico City, Mexico) 25. Joseph Lofton, Christopher Hillegas (Ellicott City, MD) 26. Ed Wall (New York, NY) 27. Rafik Armanios (Natick, MA) 28. Monika Hoffmann, Didem Durakbasa, Doris Kainacher, Omer Selcuk Baz (Vienna, Austria) 29. Rufus van den Ban, Eelco van Grootheest, Suzana Milinovic (Rotterdam, the Netherlands) 30. Peter Conant, Jessica Mann, Robert Federico, Kavita Gavandalkar, Lance Amato (New York, NY)

1. Alessandro Ayuso, William Haskis (Brooklyn, NY) 2. Elena Chernyshov, Adrian Politano (Toronto, Canada) 3. Glenn Martin (Oak Park, IL) 4. Burak Tursoy, Erkl Sahoglu, Nevter Zafer (N. Cyprus, Turkey) 5. Victoria Watson, James Madge (London, United Kingdom) 6. Nasser Amer (Newmarket, Canada) 7. Richard Farnan (Kansas City, MO) 8. Youngstar: Thomas de Bakker (Amsterdam, the Netherlands) 9. Andrew Blanda, Neil Sandvold, Christina Blumbach, Christobal Tornero (Philadelphia, PA) 10. Keiji Kanada, Asako Kawashima, Yuri Hidaka (Osaka, Japan) 11. Joshua Zinder, Ludwing Vaca (Princeton, NJ) 12. Alejandro Ogata (Kansas City, MO) 13. Mairim Dallaryan (New York, NY) 14. Joshua Atkins (Hickory Creek, TX) 15. Jerry Victorian, Mike Russell (Gainesville, FL) 16. Rick Hauser, Ali Yapicioglu, Soren Thomas, Ryan Fitzsimmons (Perry, NY) 17. Dominick A. Termini, Damian Webster (Brooklyn, NY) 18. Slimane Ouahes, Nicolas Delefosse, Gael Ribier (Paris, France) 19. Lejla Dato, Roberto Forte, Andrea Guardo (Catania, Italy) 20. Nicolas Emmanuel Enriquez, Avi Shvetz, Sam Lee (Brooklyn, NY) 21. Jim Klinkhamer, Jasper Klinkhamer (Amersfoort, the Netherlands) 22. Billy Batac, Kendra James, Brennan Stevenson (Arlington, TX) 23. Riccardo Bianchini, Federica Lusiardi (Cremona, Italy) 24. Oscar Alberto Rodriguez-Barradas, Juan Carlos Castillo-Lagrange (Caracas, Venezuela) 25. Rita Zeineddine, Tarek Ibrahim (Hamburg, Germany) 26. Susana Kyrgos, Pedro Jose Borges, Khalid Khriesat (Blacksburg, VA) 27. Adam Reed (San Antonio, TX) 28. Karlene Mootoo, Gavin McLachlan (Shanghai, China) 29. Rossana Capurso, Andrea Ricci (Brooklyn, NY) 30. Michele Adrian, Paula Meijerink, Terry Bowdoin (Newtonville, MA)

1. Jon Kershner, Jorie Garcia, Anton Henning (Muncie, IN) 2. Eduardo Rosa (London, United Kingdom) 3. Darren Zebari, Corey Campbell (Farmington Hills, MI)
4. Siobhan Burke (Los Angeles, CA) 5. Ashley Hoffman (Central, SC) 6. Davis Associates: Bruce Walker, Glenn Davis, Harold Balazs (Spokane, WA)
7. Eric Schneider (New York, NY) 8. Talia Dorsey, Abby Feldman, Andres Sevtsuk, Gabriele Evangelisti, Maia Tuur (Cambridge, MA) 9. Igor Barta (Ettlingen, Germany)
10. FPMOD: Florencia Pita (Los Angeles, CA) 11. Andres Orozco (Land O' Lakes, FL) 12. David Boyles, Jennifer Culberson, Collin Jacobs (Bozeman, MT)
13. Peter Chladek, Pavel Culek (Prague West, Czech Republic) 14. Celeste Woodfill, Irene Vogt (Houston, TX) 15. Brien Graham, Leah Byers, Julieta Porres (Dallas,
TX) 16. Edward Ingersoll, Michael Mayes (New York, NY) 17. Kary Cooper (Lubbock, TX) 18. Daniel Schwaag (London, United Kingdom) 19. Anna MacBean,
Ken Mark MacBean (Cincinnati, OH) 20. Richard Sidoroff, Larry Doane, Steve Newman, Dan Kessler, Orlando Rockwell (Denver, CO) 21. Mohamed Elnahas (Fargo, ND)
22. San Besbelli, Giancarlo Mancarella (Venice, CA) 23. Jason D. Reece (Olathe, KS) 24. Jennifer Lee, Pablo Castro, Nat Oppenheimer, Russell Davies, Shin Kang,
Kaon Ko (New York, NY) 25. Henk Bultstra, Jaakko Van't Spijker, Bert Karel Deuten (Rotterdam, the Netherlands) 26. Matthew Hironymous (Lubbock, TX)
27. Remco Arnold, Arek Seredyn (Rotterdam, the Netherlands) 28. Leal Charonnat (Oakland, CA) 29. Robert Vertes, Vaishali Patel (Brooklyn, NY)
30. Bertram Beissel, Amanda Ortland, Andrew Hartness (Minneapolis, MN)

1. Kyu Seon Hong (Suwon, Korea) 2. Sirivat Phasug (Bangkok, Thailand) 3. Justin Smith (Lubbock, TX) 4. Zoltan Pali (Los Angeles, CA) 5. Tiago Rodrigues Coelho, Amaral Bernardo (Oporto, Portugal) 6. Geoffrey Maulion (Atlanta, GA) 7. Adrian Hawker (Edinburgh, United Kingdom) 8. Arturo Bernardo, Ismaele De Rosa, Nicola Iarossi, Lauro Naclerio, Francesco Rossi (Caserta, Italy) 9. Garrett Scarborough (Gastonia, NC) 10. Thomas Kong, Susan Seah (Toronto, Canada) 11. Brian Tomlinson (St. Louis, MO) 12. Gwendolyn Wolfgang (Watkinsville, GA) 13. Team LEF: Matthew Enslin, Yang-Chyi Lee, Jeff Floyd (Flower Mound, TX) 14. TPG Architects: Armando Gallardo, Saulius Gecas, Camila Crazut, Javier Ponce (New York, NY) 15. Illiana Ivanova, Magdalena Matanova (Sofia, Bulgaria) 16. Dimosthenis Charitos (Thessaloniki, Greece) 17. Christopher Henrickson (Staten Island, NY) 18. Alison Alexander (Clemson, SC) 19. Kristin Morales, Ivan Morales, Florencia Capasso, Diego Maradei (Brooklyn, NY) 20. Brian Svedeman (Lubbock, TX) 21. Andrew Burian, Scott Schrob (Somerset, NJ) 22. Jeff Dennis, Arash Eshghpour, Eric Tang (Toronto, Canada) 23. Cory Kessler, Scott Barton (Malverne, NY) 24. Ross Anderson, MJ Sagan, Caroline Otto, Matt Greer (New York, NY) 25. Matthew Haynes (Lubbock, TX) 26. Bob Webber (Chicago, IL) 27. C3Dinteractive NA: John Aspinall, Phillip Tytler, Q. Tran (Sydney, Australia) 28. Jaewon Lee, Neda Pourshakouri, Karen Lee (Los Angeles, CA) 29. Xavier Vilalta (Barcelona, Spain) 30. Andrew So, David Helton, Edwin Carranza, Cesar Mendoza (Santa Anna Heights, CA)

1. Jean-Adrien, Paul Girard, Sophie Girard (Meudon, France) 2. Herma Heckemueller (New York, NY) 3. Rob Orcutt (Lake Worth, FL) 4. Dimitrios Diamantakos, Christos Tessas (Athens, Greece) 5. Jan Bos, Maarten Modderkolk (Voorthuizen, the Netherlands) 6. Christian Yafuso (Stillwater, OK) 7. Faraut Guillaume Anatole, Dall'ara Enrica, Mocci Chiara (La Garenne Colombes, France) 8. Daniel Day (Dallas, TX) 9. Marc Doerig, David Schloer (Alexandria, VA) 10. Francisco de la Isla, Konrad Warnholtz (Mexico City, Mexico) 11. Christopher Nicholson (Spring, TX) 12. Mary Lopez (Lewisville, TX) 13. Sebastien Queney, Sebastien Chevance (New York, NY) 14. Zorana Popic, Mitali Mandlekar (Oklahoma City, OK) 15. Matthew Helveston (Blacksburg, VA) 16. Tanya Lee, Derek Lo (Brooklyn, NY) 17. Margarita Blanco, Rita Motta, James Reilly (Aventura, FL) 18. Clint Speckmiear (Lubbock, TX) 19. Hyunjin Im (Bellevue, WA) 20. Carisa Butensky (Branchdale, PA) 21. Kristin Speth, Ashley Snell, Scott Wilson (New York, NY) 22. Claire Weisz, Mark Yoes, Brian Macintosh (New York, NY) 23. Samuli Sallinen, Jukka Savolainen, Teemu Halme (Helsinki, Finland) 24. Brendon Snyder, Mark Danser (New York, NY) 25. Options Studio, TBD: Marilu Tibana (Newark, NJ) 26. Rami Abou-Khalil (Montreal, Canada) 27. Dmytro Chornobryvets, Aleksandr Chernobrivets (Brooklyn, NY) 28. David Brown (Stillwater, OK) 29. Neelab Mahmoud (Oakland, CA) 30. Roberto Da Silva Ribeiro (Toronto, Canada)

1. Masumi Nagano, Raymond Jow (New York, NY) 2. Joerg Petri (Karlsruhe, Germany) 3. Shane Hood, Neil Chace, Dustin Siegrist, Andrew McCready, Brian Simpson, Ryan Woolard (Tulsa, OK) 4. Ferhan Azman (London, United Kingdom) 5. Yonghyun Yu (New York, NY) 6. Leslie McCool (Stillwater, OK) 7. Daekyung Jo (Cambridge, MA) 8. Hector Lo (Vancouver, Canada) 9. Margaret Kirk, Christian Rietzke (Brooklyn, NY) 10. Luca Gandini (Torino, Italy) 11. Studios GO: Gregory Okshteyn, Amanda Beethe, Tom Schonebohm, Matt Barash (New York, NY) 12. Saauda Hosein, Erika Petersen, Giovanna Brin (Miramar, FL) 13. Monica Freundt (Montreal, Canada) 14. Tal Senior (Tel Aviv, Israel) 15. Eleanor Rennie, Agnieszka Glowacka (London, United Kingdom) 16. Gary Wong (Gardena, CA) 17. Dallas Howell (Lubbock, TX) 18. Bruno Campos, Antônio Valladares (Belo Horizonte, Brazil) 19. Cynthia Galeano (Miami, FL) 20. Cassandre Pallas (Middletown, CT) 21. Rewind Arch, Dimitris Kolonis, Zetta Kotsioni (Athens, Greece) 22. David Goodman, Romina Canna (Chicago, IL) 23. Waleid Mohamed (Lake Worth, FL) 24. Marcus Long (Lubbock, TX) 25. ASPA Architectural Studio: Maciej Szarapo, Mikolaj Smolenski, Lukasz Komar, Dominika Mrozinska (Walbrzych, Poland) 26. Reid Burton (Stillwater, OK) 27. Joshua C. Coulas (Ottawa, Canada) 28. Hunter Hanahan (Seneca, SC) 29. Emre Islek, Ahmet Selim Koytak (Istanbul, Turkey) 30. Sergiu Burca (Rolling Meadows, IL)

Theaterscape!

1. Nicola Dsouza (Cincinnati, OH) 2. Barrett Feldman, Andrea Korber (New York, NY) 3. Thierry Beaudoin (Watertown, MA) 4. B. Kannan, I. Dutta, A. Zachariah (Brooklyn, NY) 5. Joel Diamant (Copenhagen, Denmark) 6. Erick Fong, Robert SooHoo (Fremont, CA) 7. Hilary Pinnington (Montreal, Canada) 8. Jason Bergeron (Vienna, Austria) 9. Woojae Kim (Cambridge, MA) 10. Zachary Emmingham, Jay-E Emmingham (Portland, OR) 11. Anna Neimark, Ying Zhou (Somerville, MA) 12. Ariff Design Consultant: Ariff Budiman Mohamad, M.Redzuan Hisham Bidin (Selangor, Malaysia) 13. Hsin-Hung Tsao (Astoria, NY) 14. Marco Basili (Rome, Italy) 15. Sarah Shipp, Roselie Enrique, Sara McCarter, Sarah Lee (Alexandria, VA) 16. John Riker, Patricia Acevedo-Riker, Martha Merzig, Josh Rodriguez (Abilene, TX) 17. Khaled Nassar (Princess Anne, MD) 18. Jacob Goldemberg, Indira Reyes, Fernando Pampolha (Rio de Janeiro, Brazil) 19. Amanda Bassiely, Jennifer Almonaci (Miami, FL) 20. Matei Senes, Tudor Timotin (Bucuresti, Romania) 21. Alexander Tauber (Vienna, Austria) 22. Guy Lafranchi, Dietmar Panzenboeck (Bern/Liebefeld, Switzerland) 23. Judith Dorlandt, Willem-Paul Dreesmann (Rotterdam, the Netherlands) 24. Natan Margulis, Eleonora Margulis, Yelena Raiko (Ness-Ziona, Israel) 25. Kevin Kernaghan (Carrollton, TX) 26. Jon Zast (Brooklyn, NY) 27. Victor Camps (Miami, FL) 28. Richard Brook, Regina Huser, Charles Burdaky (Manchester, United Kingdom) 29. Guillermo Garcia Gomez, Anne-Elisabeth Boutan (Paris, France) 30. Catherine Rothermund, Anne-Rachel Schiffmann (Brooklyn, NY)

1. **Chun Sheh Teo** (Indianapolis, IN) 2. **Naomi Schiphorst, Maarten Scheurwater** (Amsterdam, the Netherlands) 3. **Janice Wong** (Toronto, Canada) 4. **Jessica Ramirez** (Lubbock, TX) 5. **Defne Dilber, Davide Stolfi, Gianluca Brancaleone, Nicola Cabiati, Andrea Fornello, Andi Divizia** (Rome, Italy) 6. **Pell Studio: Jonathan Reisen, Ben Pell** (Instructor) (Syracuse, NY) 7. **Alain Wolff Architects: Alain Wolff, Yves Christinet, Raphaela Schacher** (Lausanne, Switzerland) 8. **Bradley Doherty** (Lubbock, TX) 9. **Pekko Eerikainen** (Vantaa, Finland) 10. **Judit Kimpian, Bettina Molnar, Laszlo Fecske** (London, United Kingdom) 11. **Justin Rice** (Lubbock, TX) 12. **Alejandro Lopez Velez, Patricio Cuello, Raul Gonzalez, Tomas Saraceno, Eduardo Luna** (Miami Beach, FL) 13. **Joshua Aronson** (Middletown, CT) 14. **Marionneau Mickael, Perron Yann, Baggio Romain** (Bordeaux, France) 15. **Juan Pable Lira, Rodrigo Piwonka, Alex Loyer** (New York, NY) 16. **Tim Fenton, Lochlan Pellew, Andres Torres Lopez** (Adelaide, Australia) 17. **Erin Newton** (Richmond, VA) 18. **Gabriel Gindel, Gabriel Benny Burstein, Dennis Alexis Tadich** (Montevideo, Uruguay) 19. **Frank Yang, Joseph Luciani, Stirling Moore, Mack Musgrave** (West Palm Beach, FL) 20. **Jordan Mussett** (Lubbock, TX) 21. **Matthias Neumann** (Brooklyn, NY) 22. **Art Balourdas, Sebastian Mariscal, Jorge Gracia, Alfonso Frade, Dominique Houriet, Jessika d'Arcy** (La Jolla, CA) 23. **Lucid Theory: Bryant Alcantara, Brian Tucker, Aamir Saeed, Jignesh Haresh** (Houston, TX) 24. **Linda Rukschcio** (Vienna, Austria)

Exhibition Curators / Editors
Jonathan Cohen-Litant and Zoë Ryan

Exhibit / Installation Design
Moorhead & Moorhead

First-place Installation Design
Kevin Carmody, Andrew Groarke, Chris Hardie,
and Lewis Kinneir

Competition Managers
Jonathan Cohen-Litant (VAI), Rachel Belsky (EDC)

Competition Associate
Marcus Woollen

VAI Project Staff
Karen Kice, Ori Topaz, Katherine Meehan, and
Ari Duraku

EDC Project Staff
Lynn Bodnar and Chirag Badlani

Competition Assistants
Linda Roby, Elizabeth Stoel, and Eva Vela

Jury Volunteers
Dana Sunshine and John Frost

VAI Interns:
Karen Chin, Jason Rosen, and Carolyn Acevedo

Competition Sponsors

Coney Island
Development Corporation

Additional Support
KeySpan Energy
The Independence Community Foundation

Competition Jury
Carol Hill Albert, Co-owner of Astroland Park
Paola Antonelli, Curator, Department of Architecture
    and Design, Museum of Modern Art
Jon Benguiat, Director of Planning and Development,
    Brooklyn Borough President's Office
Charles Denson, Author, *Coney Island Lost and
    Found* (Ten Speed Press, 2002)
Mark Hacker, Director of Development,
    Rockwell Group
Michael A. Manfredi, Partner, Weiss/Manfredi
    Architects
Cynthia Reich, Deputy Director, New York Aquarium
Sheryl Robertson, Coney Island resident and
    local community organizer
Jennifer Siegal, Principal and founder, Office of
    Mobile Design
Joshua J. Sirefman, CIDC Chair, Director of Mayor's
    Office of Economic Development & Rebuilding
Julius Spiegel, Brooklyn Borough Commissioner,
    New York City Department of Parks and
    Recreation